The Man Who Hunted
Jack the Ripper

The Man Who Hunted
Jack the Ripper

Nicholas Connell & Stewart P. Evans

AMBERLEY

First published in 2000 by Rupert Books

This edition first published 2012

Amberley Publishing
The Hill, Stroud
Gloucestershire, GL5 4EP

www.amberley-books.com

British Library Cataloguing in Publication Data.
A catalogue record for this book is available from the British Library.

ISBN 978-1-4456-0827-3

Typesetting and Origination by Amberley Publishing.
Printed in Great Britain.

Contents

List of Illustrations

13. Reid in 1888. (*Illustrated Police News*)
14. Yard at rear of 29 Hanbury Street. (Authors' collection)
15. Church Passage, Aldgate, looking towards murder site. (Robin Odell)
16. Reid attending Elizabeth Stride's inquest. (*Penny Illustrated Paper*)
17. Church Passage, Aldgate, from Mitre Square. (Robin Odell)
18. George Hutchinson observing Mary Kelly and a client on the night of her murder. (Authors' collection)
19. Arrest of a Jewish suspect. (Authors' collection)
20. Map showing the locations of the Whitechapel murders. (Authors' collection)
21. Sergeant Stephen White. (*Lloyd's Weekly Newspaper*)
22. PC William Pennett who discovered the Pinchin Street Torso. (Authors' collection)
23. Reid and Sergeant William Thick at the time of Alice McKenzie's murder. (*Illustrated Police News*)
24. Inspector William Nixon Race. (*Police Review and Parade Gossip*)
25. James Thomas Sadler. (Authors' collection)
26. Chief Constable Sir Melville Macnaghten. (Metropolitan Police)
27. Reid's son-in-law Sergeant Thomas Smith, Whitechapel Division. (Metropolitan Police)
28. John Canham Read, the Southend murderer. (*Illustrated Police News*)
29. Detective Inspector Edmund Reid, 1896. (*Police Review and Parade Gossip*)
30. Severin Klosowski, alias George Chapman, the Borough poisoner. (*Shurey's Illustrated*)
31. Dr Thomas Neill Cream, the Lambeth poisoner. (Authors' collection)
32. The Lower Red Lion, Herne. (Harold Gough)
33. Reid's Ranch with its owner standing at the gate. (Harold Gough)
34. The Hampton-on-Sea Hotel. Reid in retirement selling postcards and lemonade. (Harold Gough)
35. Reid frequently aired his views in national and local newspapers. (*Lloyd's Weekly News*)
36. George Joseph Smith, the Brides in the Bath murderer. (Authors' collection)
37. Reid on the bridge over the 'Lavender Brook.' (Harold Gough)
38. Summer concerts at Herne Bay. (Authors' collection)

Acknowledgements

The authors wish to thank the staff of the British Library, British Library Newspaper Library, Canterbury Cathedral Archives, Centre for Kentish Studies, East Kent Archives Centre, Herne Bay Library, London Metropolitan Archives, Metropolitan Police Archive Department, Metropolitan Police Museum, the National Archives, Southwark Local History Library and Tower Hamlets Local History Library.

Also thanks to Peter Day, Rosemarie Evans, Raymond Godfrey, the late Stuart Goffee, the late Harold Gough, the late Melvin Harris, Robin Odell, Jon Ogan, Maggie Ramsden, Don Rumbelow, Keith Skinner, R. Dixon Smith, Phil Sugden, Kate Thompson and Richard Whittington-Egan.

Introduction

by Richard Whittington-Egan

In the year of Our Lord—and of the Antithetic Devil—1888, there flitted through the gloom and glimmer of pea-soup-fogged Whitechapel and its adjunctive parishes not only wraithlike, blood-hungry Jack but also a confused and confusing host of those who followed bret-hot upon his clean-pared heels: a vast company—Metropolitan and City—of 'blue-bottles' pursui-vant.

The tale of this red-flagged chase has oftentimes been told, but never, I think, heretofore with the breviate clarity achieved in this book, which, moreover and most unusually, has something distinctly novel to add to the curl-edged, time-crimped narrative.

For once, the hero—anti-hero perhaps, to be pedantic—is not the sly, triumphant, Victorian bogey-man, Jack, but the hunter rather than the hunted.

From long ascription, the one police officer whose name and image instantly rise Ripperwise is Inspector Frederick George Abberline. In fact, he was merely the tip rather than the top of the investigatory iceberg. There was another. One who should rank at least as high—in many respects higher—than Abberline on the roll. His name, known to all serious students of the case, albeit remembered by a mere handful of those either more dedicated or else nature-endowed with better memories, is Edmund Reid, Detective Inspector, and, at the culminal cataclysmic hour, the man who, at the cutting edge, fine-combed the highways, byways, gutters, pubs, doss-houses and brothels for increasingly phantasmagoric-seeming Jack.

What did we know of Reid? Virtually nothing. What do we know of him now? Virtually everything—thanks to the researches carried out by the authors of this book. It is all, for the first time, gathered and docketed here. More than that, here, also for the first time, are set out with absolute lucidity the names, locations, and responsibilities of each of the police officers at every stage and level—a link-by-link exposition of the chain of command of those who took contemporary and official part in the Great Ripper Hunt. And in the process of the construction of this ordinal, our authors provide a beautifully clear-lined and neatly articulated account, shorn of all accumulations of obliterative dross, of the sequences of the controversially ascribed original quintet of Ripperine murders, as well as of the additional quinary of even more dubitably Ripper-stamped homicides.

Now as to Reid himself, *qua* a person. Born a man of Kent, within the melodious parish of Canterbury bells, above a Pickfords office in quaint-named Beer Cart Lane, he was removed early in his life pilgrimage to London—Pickwickian Southwark—where he grew up.

After a somewhat chequered start—praeludial kaleidoscope of juvenile odd jobs succeeded by serious trials in seventeen trades—in the harsh, adult world of daily bread winning, he presented himself, in 1872, at the—in his case ripely experienced—age of twenty-six for enlistment in the ranks of the Metropolitan Police and, although lacking in the statutory requirement of stature, was accepted, inches discounted, to become the shortest standing man in the force.

He had found his true milieu. His reputation rose rapidly, like the balloons in which it was his unusual hobby to ascend. But, surely, he achieved the greatest height of his career with his feet firmly on the ground, the killing ground of London's East End 1888. It was in the July of 1887 that he had come to that quarter, replacing, as head of H (Whitechapel) Division C.I.D., Inspector Abberline, who had been uplifted to Scotland Yard.

Since Reid was practically involved, although, admittedly, in varying degrees, in all the Ripper investigations, excluding those of the despatch of Mary Ann Nichols in J Division and Catherine Eddowes, which took place on City of London Police ground, but including those three further highly questionably Ripperine peradventurings, 'Clay Pipe' Alice McKenzie, the enigmatic affair of the Pinchin Street torso, and the dubiously Jack-knifed Frances Coles. His views make important reading. The authors have canvassed and culled those views for us extremely carefully and conscientiously. They constitute an important part of the book.

Scattered, too, throughout the text of this undoubtedly most valuable volume are *bonnes bouches* of new information. There is, for instance, provision of a convincing genesis of the elusive—illusive—'Fairy Fay'; there is a possible identification—the authors disavow dogma—of Mary Jane Kelly's 'Morganstone'; there is a recently rediscovered, free-speaking interview with Dr Percy Clark, Dr George Bagster Phillips' assistant, who, after his principal's death in 1897, took over the practice at No. 2 Spital Square, Spitalfields; there is a significant newly recovered letter to the Editor of the *Daily Chronicle* from Albert Bachert, he of the old Whitechapel Vigilance Committee, opining regarding the murder of Frances Coles.

Quite aside from the fascination of the account of Reid's professional part in the futile, as it proved, struggle to capture and cage the Whitechapel murderer, eight of whose putative killings had taken place on Reid's 'manor', the inspector is himself a character well worth reading about. In his private life he was given to such pursuits as parachuting from a balloon at the height of 1,000 feet. He was a member of the Ancient Order of Druids and was also voted Grand Noble Arch of the New Order of the Prince Bismarck Lodge.

In his professional life he earned himself the crown of 'King of the Capturers of Coiners', as well as the distinction of being the officer of the law who, in the year of the Ripper, brought the perpetrators of the celebrated Great Silk Robberies of that time to justice.

He retired in 1896, early, due to persistent ill-health. Even in retirement, he found himself, he confessed, haunted by the horror of the unsolved Whitechapel murders and remained convinced to the end of his days that the Ripper was a terrible mad creature, who, by 1896, had been dead for some years.

Reid lost his wife of thirty-two years, Emily, in August 1900. She died, confined at the end in an asylum, of chronic organic brain disease. The widower moved to Hampton-on-Sea, a tiny hamlet a mile and a half west of Herne Bay. As old age enfolded him, he sank into the swaddling clothes of smiling, senile eccentricity. He bought a house, which he painted with crenellated battlements and protruding cannons, named it 'Reid's Ranch', and moved in with a pet parrot for company, and from a shed at the bottom of his garden, designated by him the Hampton-on-Sea Hotel, he, white-bearded and portly now, sold lemonade and picture postcards. There he lived under the ever-increasing serious threat of coastal erosion of vanishing—house, parrot and all—into the hungry sea.

He abandoned the Ranch in 1916, before the sea could have him, and backtracked to Herne Bay, where—but not before taking another bride—he succumbed to cerebral haemorrhage on 5 December 1917.

Edmund Reid's own eloquent testimony in regard to the identity of Slippery Jack: 'I challenge anyone to produce a tittle of evidence of any kind against anyone. The earth has been raked over and the seas have been swept, to find this criminal 'Jack the Ripper', always without success.'

Indeed, the Augean sweeping and Herculean raking have been disturbing the dust and earth these hundred years and more now. Dedicated phalanxes of crime historians have, with positively Sherlockian devotion, scrutinised every facet of the Ripper mystery—many employing the magnifying glass of their imagination. A good deal has been achieved. Quite a mass of material—not all strictly relevant—has been rescued from the yawning maw of oblivion. But, like the categories of negligence in the law of tort, the tortuosities of this unique case are never closed. There are still 'windows' of opportunity, such as the fenestration here pierced and furnished by Nicholas Connell and Stewart Evans, remaining in need of penetration and adornment.

Betraying in its easy style nothing of the difficulties, the persistent industry, the unremitting demands of research necessitated by the putting of it together, the authors of this pioneering biographical enterprise are to be congratulated upon the resounding success of its achievement.

'There are cleverer men than Sherlock Holmes at Scotland Yard to-day. Among these was one of the most remarkable men of the century, Edmund Reid.'

Weekly Dispatch, 8 March 1896

'If Mr. Reid were to write his reminiscences I believe many would be much delighted in reading them.'

Herne Bay Press, 29 October 1910

CHAPTER ONE

The Making of a Police Officer

> 'My boyhood was passed in efforts to find something for which I was fitted, and in the meantime earning my livelihood.'
>
> Edmund Reid

Edmund John James Reid was born on 21 March 1846 in Beer Cart Lane, Canterbury, Kent, above a Pickfords Removals office.[1] The registrar recorded on his birth certificate the exact minute of his arrival into the world, 12.15 a.m. This often indicates that the infant was one half of a set of twins but not in Reid's case. Named after his maternal grandfather, Edmund Driver, a Kentish gentleman, Reid's Scottish father was John Reid, a railway clerk, and his mother Martha Elizabeth Olivia Driver, of Southwark. John had married Martha whilst working in London.

The family moved to London living, again above a Pickfords office, in Hunter Street. They also resided at York Terrace, Southwark and then the Victoria Arms, Camberwell, with Reid's five sisters, Martha, Flora, Jessie, Mary and Marian. As soon as Reid was old enough to work he earned money by buying copies of the *Times* newspaper and hiring them out for a penny an hour. This was then a common practice and Reid recalled another, 'a man who made a living by lending papers on the day of issue and selling them outright at half price the day following.'

He then worked as a grocer's delivery boy for a Mr Hughs, whose shop was in the Walworth Road. One of his duties 'was to carry bags containing a quarter of a hundredweight of sugar (lump dust as it was called) for an old gentleman named White who kept a grocer's shop in Thurloe Street. He used to make 'stone' ginger beer in the washhouse, and many a glass he has given me for carrying the sugar. That old gentleman was the first Mr White, the founder of the great firm that is now a limited liability company, with vans all over London.'[2] R. White's, of course, are now famous for their lemonade.

During a spell working as a hotel waiter in 1868, Reid returned to Canterbury to marry Emily Jane Wilson, the daughter of a labourer at the Canterbury Baptist Chapel, on her twenty-second birthday. They returned to Southwark and eventually two children were born: Elizabeth in 1873, and Harold in 1882.

Upon getting married, Reid continued to seek his vocation in life and tried seventeen trades in all, at each of which he claimed to be proficient. These included pastry cook and steward on a 'Husband's (or Hat's) boat', a fast steamer running from London Bridge to Margate on Saturday afternoons to carry London workers to their wives, who were on holiday in Margate whilst their men folk worked. The boats maintained well-stocked bars, and the stewards did their best to relieve the men of their hard-earned pay with some success, much to the annoyance of their wives. As a result the boats had a reputation for rowdiness.

Finally Reid found his calling in life, a job that was to engage him for over twenty-three years and offered the variety he desired. On 4 November 1872, he joined the Metropolitan Police Force. He was given Warrant number 56100[3] and initially stationed at Carter Street, Walworth. PC P478 Reid was the shortest man in the Met at only five feet six inches. Although the minimum height requirement was five feet eight inches, this ruling had been relaxed for a couple of weeks because of a manpower shortage. Still a half an inch below the new minimum, Reid was accepted, as 'coming from the boats I was healthy and strong, and the Chief Inspector, who was in charge, said it did not matter.'[4]

The Metropolitan Police Force of those days, and their method of policing, included many practices and traditions that survived into late twentieth-century policing. Notably the rank structure, divisions and the foot patrol system remained very similar. In 1888, the year of the Jack the Ripper murders, the Metropolitan Police Force, during the daytime, covered the ordinary beats with some 1,561 men with an additional 522 constables stationed on 'fixed points' between 9.00 a.m. to 1.00 a.m. (thus allowing the public to know where to find a constable if they needed one). About 80 more officers were detailed to attend hackney-carriage stands. Urban day duty was normally sixteen hours divided into four reliefs (4 hours on and 4 hours off) commencing at 6.00 a.m. and ending at 10.00

p.m. On night duty the hours of work commenced at 10.00 p.m. and lasted until 6.00 a.m. Sixty per cent of available police worked on this watch. A month's day duty was succeeded by two month's night duty and a roster was posted in each police station by which the hours of each man could be ascertained. There was an allowance that if pressure of work necessitated it, leave of every kind could be suspended and the working of the beats duly organized to meet emergencies.

Throughout Sir Charles Warren's reign as Commissioner (1886-1888) the standard of education and physique of police recruits was raised. Metropolitan police constables came from all parts of England excepting the extreme north where they were mainly attracted to Liverpool, Leeds, Manchester and Glasgow. Provincial recruits were generally recognised to be in better physical condition than Londoners. It is amusing to note that recruits from the provinces were said to have more robust appetites than their London counterparts to the degree that when Londoners outnumbered the provincial recruits in the section house the food expenditure was lower. A police constable was required to 'keep up sufficient knowledge of drill in order to enable him to march in file from one street to another, or to form up quickly in times of procession and on fête days, in order to line the streets.' In the September 1888 quarter there was an average of eight drill days with an average of 3,500 men attending. This was the equivalent to two hours' drill per man per quarter, although the September quarter involved the longest drill. Mindful of the incorrect criticism that the press levelled at Warren for drilling the police it should be noted that during 1886 and 1887 drill was almost entirely given up. The Metropolitan Police discarded the old police rattles in 1884, which were replaced with whistles. A cape was issued to each constable for wet weather use.

Police constables walked their beats at the regulation pace of two-and-a-half miles per hour and the average beat length all over the Metropolitan district was seven and a half miles for day duty and two miles for night duty. In heavily populated areas the beats were much shorter. A register was kept of all beats. By day the constables kept to the kerb side of the pavement but by night they kept to the inner side to facilitate the ease of checking bolts and fastenings of houses and business premises with their bull's-eye lanterns.

Reid spent his first two years in uniform, and this included a stint on traffic duty at the Elephant and Castle. Just over two years after joining, Reid was promoted to P Division's Detective Department.[5] He 'always made it a point to dress smartly'[6] and four years later was promoted to third-class sergeant in the Criminal Investigation Department.[7] Although the height restrictions in the C.I.D. were more lax, at five feet seven inches, the Chief Commissioner was able to waive this with the Home Secretary's permission, and Reid met the other requirements of his new position, having served for over two years in uniform and being aged between twenty-seven and thirty-five years.[8]

Reid distinguished himself as a detective officer, and an early success was the arrest of a prolific burglar, Frederick George Barton, in 1876. The offender was sentenced to ten years' penal servitude and Reid moved on to his next case.[9] In 1877 he captured three horse thieves, James Dickenson, Charles Dalton and Charles Chumbley, and the former two were convicted, receiving seven years each in prison.[10] Reid was recommended for promotion in February 1880 and went for an interview and examinations in Westminster. He then became a sergeant first-class.[11] Five years later he was made a second-class inspector and transferred to Scotland Yard.[12] Reid was the last inspector to be appointed by Sir Howard Vincent, the first-ever head of the C.I.D.[13]

As Reid's professional reputation grew he enjoyed a parallel 'career' as a character in a series of novels by his old friend, the Scottish author Charles Gibbon, whose work was reputed to be a favourite of Queen Victoria's. Gibbon reversed Reid's name and portrayed him as the good-natured Detective Sergeant Dier. His description of 'Dier' was deemed to be very true to life according to those who knew Reid:

> He had obtained the services of a detective who possessed the highest qualifications for his office, namely, he was not like a detective at all in manner, appearance or speech. Meeting Sergeant Dier in an ordinary way, you would regard him as a successful commercial man. There was not the slightest flavour of Scotland Yard about him. He was a good actor, a good singer, and a capital story-teller. Some of his most important discoveries were made whilst he was entertaining a roomful of company with his merry anecdotes. The secret of his success lay partly in a natural gift for his business, his enthusiasm, and the good-nature which underlay it all. He never allowed a scoundrel to escape; but he dealt very gently with any poor creature who might be betrayed into a first crime.
>
> Sergeant Dier was waiting for him. Anyone looking at the detective as he stood, bareheaded, reading a newspaper, would have imagined that he was one of the bank officials.

Sergeant Dier bowed and left. Outside the room he nodded and smiled to himself as he placed a glossy hat on his head. Mentally and cheerfully he was saying: 'I don't care about that chap—not much. I should not be surprised to find him coming my way some time with the positions changed.'[14]

Ill-health and bad luck blighted Gibbon's happy family life. Much of his fortune was lost through the failure of a banking firm and a gas explosion at his home in 1880 left him with severe burns and shock from which he never fully recovered. He died in 1890 at the early age of forty-seven[15] and this must have been a blow to Reid, who saw the popular author as 'almost a brother'. Years later Reid showed a visitor to his home the references to Detective Dier in his collection of Gibbon's books, 'references too, of a distinctly flattering nature. It was proof positive of the ex-detective's abilities and the high standing to which he had attained in his profession.'[16]

As if his work did not provide him with enough excitement and danger, Reid's hobby of ballooning surely did. He started ballooning shortly after joining the police force and was once described as 'the most daring balloonist of the early eighties.'[17] In the 1870s he made a parachute jump from a balloon at the height of 1,000 feet at a Luton fête and in 1883 he was awarded a gold medal in commemoration of his record ascent in the balloon Queen of the Meadow.[18] During his police career Reid made twenty-three balloon ascents from Crystal Palace and Alexandra Palace.[19]

CHAPTER TWO

East End Detective

'I am a police officer, I shall apprehend you for attempting to kill your wife.'

Edmund Reid

Reid was transferred from A (Central) Division and appointed Local Inspector, C.I.D., in the newly formed J (Bethnal Green) Division in the East End of London on 31 July 1886, three days before the Division became operational.[1] The local inspectors (such as Reid) and their men dealt with most routine crime in the divisions in the C.I.D., including cases of murder. Scotland Yard would usually become involved only when it was an unusual or serious case. Within a matter of weeks Reid took charge of a major investigation.

John Reynolds, thirty-two years old, lived with his wife of nine years, Sarah Ann, and their five children at 43 Globe Road, Mile End. He was perceived by those who knew him as a man 'who displayed every affection for his family, and was held in general respect.' Around the start of 1886 Reynolds became a barman at The George and Vulture in Tottenham, where he lived on the premises under the pretence of being a single man, which was his usual practice and one his wife was aware of. For over two years the young and attractive Emma Ship had worked at the pub as cook and housemaid. Reynolds and Ship soon became close and he helped her to write letters to her mother, as 'she was no scholar'. Reynolds proposed to Ship who accepted after considering the matter for a week. He gave her a brooch and measured her finger for a ring, although she never received one. He even visited Emma at her mother's house in Grange Road, Plaistow, where he was introduced as her future son-in-law.

Things soured at the pub, however, when another barman complained of the quality of his food and accused Emma of giving Reynolds preferential treatment and better food. The landlady agreed and dismissed Emma, as she was 'keeping company' with Reynolds. He in turn resigned and was unemployed for about a month. His wife recalled that 'since then I have lived very unhappily with him—that arose from him going out and leaving me so many hours, which he had never done before—he had lived on good terms with me before that.'

Reynolds soon took up the position of barman at The Lucas Arms in the Grays Inn Road, where he lived with another barman, Percy Stapleton. Reynolds made weekly visits to Emma at her mother's house and they corresponded regularly. He signed his letters to her, 'Your truly beloved and affectionate lover, G. Reynolds' (he had told her that his name was George). She signed her letters to him, 'Your most truly affectioned beloved intended, E. Ship'. The result of this liaison was that Reynolds obtained some sulphate of copper, otherwise known as Bluestone, an emetic poison easily found at grocers' and chemists, and attempted to poison his wife.

Sarah Reynolds still received occasional visits from her wayward husband and it appeared that their relationship was improving. On 17 August she opened a letter from Reynolds inviting her on a day trip to the coastal resort of Southend in Essex the following day. Reynolds signed off 'with my kind love, from your truly beloved and affectionate husband, J.R.' The couple travelled by train to Southend, dined on roast mutton, potatoes and beans opposite the beach, went for a walk and had their portraits taken. Sarah also ate half-a-dozen oysters, the fifth of which tasted 'very nasty.' She felt ill on the boat back to London and was sick after drinking some stout.

Upon returning home, Reynolds suggested a cup of spruce and peppermint might make Sarah feel better. He made it for her but when Sarah tried to take the cup Reynolds stopped her saying she should have it when she went to bed. Reynolds then groomed his moustache with a clothes brush and took Sarah to her sister's house despite her still feeling very ill. He left Sarah after reminding her to drink the spruce and peppermint which she did even though it tasted unpleasant.

Within minutes Sarah's heart started beating faster and she felt such intense pain that she put a finger down her throat to induce vomiting. Upon examining the cup she saw a quantity of blue substance in the bottom of it. Sarah made herself sick again and spent a restless night suffering from pain round her heart and stomach.

The following day she received a letter from her husband:

Dear Wife

Just to say I got home quite safe last night, but I am sorry to say that I do not feel very well to-day: also, my dear, I hope and trust that you are better then you was last night when I left you. I felt quite miserable thinking that I should have to leave you as you was so poorly. My dear wife, you mite drop me a few line to say how you are, as I am very queer myself; wonder if it was those oysters that upset us. It must have been something to do it, as we was allright before we had them. So I must conclued with my kind love, from your truly beloved and affectionate husband.

J. Reynolds

Sarah remembered that her husband had not complained of being ill after eating the oysters and had eaten supper on returning home which she had been unable to do. There must have been some suspicion in her mind for she had the sediment in the cup examined by a local chemist. The poisonous content was discovered and Sarah Ann repaired to the local police station, where she saw Inspector Reid. Reid took up the investigation and saw the chemist, who informed him that the drink had contained sulphate of copper, or Bluestone, a fast-acting poison.

Reid went to The Lucas Arms with PC Williamson, where he arrested Reynolds for the attempted murder of his wife. Reynolds denied the charge, and Reid went with Percy Stapleton to Reynolds' room. There he found a small amount of cash and something blue wrapped in a piece of paper. He returned to the room with Reynolds and pointed out the paper containing the blue substance before directly accusing Reynolds, who stated that he had not seen it before, did not know what bluestone was and was innocent of the charge. Reid recorded Reynold's answers in his memorandum book. It was his practice to not say much and just note the answers, not the questions he put.

Years later Reid outrageously embellished his recollection arresting Reynolds: 'He gave me a fine doing, too. We fell down six flights of stairs together, and had a fresh struggle on every landing. He fought hard for his freedom. But I had him safe.'[2]

Reynolds was taken to Bethnal Green Police Station and there a letter from Emma was found in his possession. Reid gathered his evidence and

Reynolds, who was quickly found guilty, received a sentence of twenty years at his Old Bailey trial. The judge described the case as one of the 'innumerable instances in human history that misguided and uncontrolled passion led people to the commission of crimes of the deepest dye. Any crime blacker or more atrocious it was difficult to conceive.' The arrest and conviction of the poisoner greatly enhanced Reid's reputation.[3] Afterwards he arranged a benefit concert for Sarah Reynolds at the Kay Street Radical Club.[4]

Detective Inspector Reid became a well-known and respected figure in the East End of London, and the following newspaper report paid tribute to him:

[a] self-made man, who in 14 years has raised himself—we say raised himself, because he had only his own brains to help him—from the position of fourth class constable in the P division, through the grades of third, second, and first-class constable, and sergeant to that of Chief [sic] Inspector of Detectives in the J or Bethnal Green Division. He has been engaged in some of the most difficult cases in recent years; and his functions now in the East End are to take charge of a staff of officers belonging to the Criminal Investigation Department. The importance of such a position is great; because cases presented by the poor and uneducated, or which, through artifices resorted to, would often pass as trivial, are carefully watched for those features, which, when examined, often lead up to the discovery of the actual offenders. East Enders will recollect the attempt made by the barman of a tavern in the Grays-Inn-Road to poison his wife, then living in Globe Road, Mile End. Largely owing to the skill and experience of this officer, a notorious rascal received the punishment due to the offence—20 years' penal servitude.

The eulogy ended by saying that 'anyone requiring advice will find inspector Reid at his office, Police Station, Bethnal Green Road, courteous, ready, and willing to furnish to applicants any information or assistance in his power.'[5] At a time when the Metropolitan Police, in general, were receiving much criticism and were suffering the barbs of the press, Reid escaped such personal embarrassment. The satirical paper, *Toby*, commented that 'were it not for a little individuality displayed by some officers, few criminals would be brought to justice,' and the piece was accompanied by a cartoon of 'a clever East End detective Inspector Reid' riding a donkey representing Scotland Yard.[6]

Despite his apparent success, Reid's tenure at Bethnal Green was relatively short. On 30 July 1887, he received a reprimand from the head of the C.I.D., Assistant Commissioner James Monro, and was immediately transferred to neighbouring H (Whitechapel) Division.[7] Although the contemporary Police Orders do not specify the nature of his misconduct, the offence must have been minor, as he retained his rank and level of pay. In his new post as local inspector of H Division Reid had a difficult act to follow. He replaced a hugely experienced officer who had held the post for fourteen years and was now being transferred to the Central Office at Scotland Yard. He was Detective Inspector Frederick George Abberline. Abberline, who would eventually earn eighty-four commendations and rewards, was highly regarded. Even the satirical *Toby* had the following to say of Abberline: 'A well known East Ender, and also very well known for his official and private virtues. So enamoured is he of his fellow creatures, that scores of persons are indebted to him. He has a decent amount of curiosity, and has been known to stop gentlemen at the most unholy times and places and enquire most affectionately about their health and work—questions which are often settled by a magistrate, generally in Mr Abberline's favour.'[8]

A dinner and presentation for Abberline was held at The Unicorn Tavern, High Street, Shoreditch, in December 1887, where appreciation was shown for fourteen years in the service of the local community. He was presented with a beautiful gold keyless hunting watch and a purse filled with gold. On the watch was engraved the following:

Presented, together with a purse of gold, to Inspector F.G. Abberline by the inhabitants of Spitalfields, Whitechapel, etc., on his leaving the district after fourteen years' service, as a mark of their esteem and regard.—G. HAY YOUNG, Chairman; J.C. MCDONALD, Hon. Sec.

Abberline, in responding, said that:

he could hardly find language sufficient to express his thanks to the chairman for his too flattering expressions, and to the company present for the honour they did him that evening, and for the beautiful and substantial testimonial of their goodwill presented to him by the chairman in their behalf. He assured them that he was deeply indebted to them for the many kindnesses he had received during the 14 years he was with them. He felt sorry to leave the district, but he was getting into years, and an opportunity occurred that did not occur every day. He accepted a call to the head office, Great Scotland Yard, with a view of bettering his prospects.[9]

Abberline departed the familiar streets of Whitechapel and the East End in general and moved on to the next stage of his distinguished career, at Scotland Yard. At 10.00 a.m. on 1 August 1887, Inspector Reid started work in Whitechapel and set about supervising detectives of the busiest division in the East End.[10]

CHAPTER THREE

⟶1888

'It has some of the smartest men attached to its CID. I need only mention the name of Detective Reid as an instance of that.'

Superintendent Thomas Arnold

The year 1888 saw a marked rise in crime generally and the murders in Whitechapel were to necessitate the concentration of large bodies of police in particular localities. Such an increase in force could be achieved only by diminishing the number of men ordinarily employed in other divisions. Furthermore, it was at a time that the force was being overworked. There were 200 police stations of various sorts in the Metropolitan area, their character generally determined by the position of the site. During 1888 new stations were completed and opened at Forest Gate, Surbiton, Canning Town, and Chingford. Works for new stations were in progress at New Southgate, Tooting, Limehouse and Finchley. Some stations were old houses that had once been the residence of merchants for example, that were converted into quarters for the police, such as that in Leman Street, headquarters of Whitechapel Division. Bow Street and Commercial Street stations were examples of large stations that were the vogue prior to 1880.

In 1888 a constable entering the force started at 24s. per week, with clothing. This rose until after about eight years' service he received £78 per annum. These amounts were subject to deductions for pension and about 2d. per week to gratuity funds for the widows and orphans of deceased comrades. Sergeants were paid 34s. per week for the first two years, rising to 36s. for the next three and then 38s. There were three grades of inspector at £187. Divisional Superintendents, such as Thomas Arnold in Whitechapel, commenced at £300 rising £10 annually to £475. Reserve men received extra pay of 1s. 6d. per week for constables, 3s. per week for sergeants and 4s. for inspectors. Allowances for special duty ranged from 2s. to 19s. 2d. per week.[1]

The Metropolitan Police Force was (and is) the largest in the country and numbered 14,261 men in 1888. About 1,600 were permanently engaged on special duties in various government departments, including special-protection posts at public offices and buildings, dockyards, and military stations. With a total yearly expenditure of over £1.5 million (a huge amount in 1888), the Metropolitan Police were always operating on a tight budget. The government supplied £572,000 for pay and clothing alone. With 75,000 arrests yearly, plus 1,000 fires attended by police, 134,000 summonses served, 6,300 people taken to hospital, as well as other police duties, they were kept very busy.[2] Whitechapel, including Spitalfields, was the heartland of the roughest police territory in the whole of the metropolis.

It is hard to imagine, especially for someone living outside London, that this area, even then, was a seething mass of immigrants of all nationalities and religions; visiting seamen, soldiers from the nearby barracks (the Tower of London was a short walk away), beggars, street traders, and performers; prostitutes, down and outs, visiting theatre and pub-goers, and sightseers. The latter included 'slumming toffs' who enjoyed seeing 'how the other half lived' and punters seeking the favours of the numerous streetwalkers. Far from being noticed, a stranger was the norm in this area. Contrary to popular belief, the main thoroughfares were not quiet after midnight but were busily populated the whole night long, not only by the homeless but also by late and early workers, coffee stall customers and many others from the populace. The population of Whitechapel and St George's-in-the-East alone numbered over 110,000, and these all lived in H Division. By 1888 Tower Hamlets was an overcrowded ghetto of displaced workers with shelter at a premium. Those who sub-let in turn sub-let to others.

On the night of 2 April 1888, Emma Elizabeth Smith, a 42-year-old prostitute living in lodgings at 18 George Street, Spitalfields, was seen talking to a man dressed in dark clothes and white scarf at 12.15 a.m. She returned to her lodgings between 4 and 5 a.m. (on the 3rd) and stated that she had been assaulted and robbed in Osborn Street, on the pathway opposite 10 Brick Lane, about 300 yards from her lodgings. Smith was walked to the London Hospital, a distance of about half a mile, where she was examined and it was found that a blunt instrument, which had been thrust up her vagina, had penetrated her peritoneum. She also had bruising to her head and her right ear was torn. Smith was detained in the hospital, where she died at 9 a.m. on 4 April, of peritonitis. The only description she was able to give of her attackers was that there were three of them, one aged about 19, and that she was attacked while passing Whitechapel Church.

The case was not immediately reported to the police, who became aware only when the coroner's officer reported it on the 6th. The inquiry regarding this murder was then handed over to Inspector Reid, who attended the inquest. No police officers on duty in the area had seen or heard anything on what had been an otherwise quiet night and no offenders were traced. The mystery surrounding Emma Smith's murder was to add to the sensation of press stories later that year. It was also to play a part in the creation of a fictional Jack the Ripper victim, christened in 1950 but with roots in 1888—'Fairy Fay'.

'Fairy Fay', the apocryphal murder victim, has both intrigued and baffled historians of the Whitechapel murders for many years. In fact the appearance of this unknown victim was first mooted in September 1888, when the Whitechapel murders first became recognised as a 'series'. The victim was variously stated to have been murdered during 'Christmas week' 1887 or on Boxing Day 1887. At this time she was nameless.

In 1950 the unknown victim was given a name. Journalist Terence Robertson called her 'Fairy Fay', and his article marks the first appearance of this appellation. Robertson was writing a series of articles about the cases of Scotland Yard, in *Reynolds News*, entitled 'CALL IN THE YARD'. The story entitled, 'MADMAN WHO MURDERED NINE WOMEN', marked Robertson's excursion into Jack the Ripper research. Not unnaturally a source of information for him was the archives of *Reynolds News*.

As research into these murders became more serious, most responsible writers and researchers realised that 'Fairy Fay' was indeed apocryphal and was somehow a press creation born of the murder of Emma Elizabeth Smith. But it still puzzled and attracted the attention of this new generation. The records were scoured, but no trace of a murder victim at the requisite time could be found. The semi-legendary status of 'Fairy Fay' grew, and the name appeared in many books. No murder, however, was recorded in Whitechapel for that month.

To fully address the problem we must return to that 1950 article in *Reynolds News*. What exactly did Robertson say? As his title implied, he deduced that Jack the Ripper had nine victims. But who was the first? It couldn't be Emma Smith, as her attackers were stated to have been a gang and not a solitary individual. Robertson failed to mention her at all in his piece. He says, however, 'The appalling murders he committed between Christmas 1887, and September, 1889', thus showing the series to have begun with an 'unreported' murder and ended with the Pinchin Street torso case of 10 September 1889. The story is told in typical sensational style, the journalese flowing freely. Then comes the first of Robertson's wonderful inventions: 'First victim in this ghastly parade of death was a woman known as 'Fairy Fay', for want of a better name' [authors' emphasis]. There is the crucial phrase: 'for want of a better name.' Robertson here is clearly stating that he has invented the name. The name 'Fairy Fay' almost certainly originated from the popular song 'Polly Wolly Doodle' in which 'Fairy Fay' is a wanton or abandoned woman.[3]

He continued:

On the cold Boxing Night of 1887, she decided to take a short cut home from a pub in Mitre Square. This decision, which took her through the dim alleyways behind Commercial Road, cost her her life.

Two hours after she set out, a constable, on beat [sic] shone his flickering oil lamp into a darkened doorway. At the inquest he said his lamp revealed a sight which sickened him.

In its ray was all that was left of 'Fairy Fay.'

Inspector Reid of Commercial Road [sic] police station, took charge. His detectives questioned dozens of people who lived in the drab house overlooking the scene of the crime.

After a few weeks of vain inquiries, Inspector Reid informed his chief at Metropolitan Police Headquarters, New Scotland Yard [sic], that the case had been shelved.

Only brief reports of the murder appeared in the Press, and by February the case was forgotten.[4]

Robertson then moved on to the case of Martha Turner (also called Tabram) as being the next in the series. Thus the December 1887 victim was born, set to baffle researchers for years to come. Some merely accepted her as the first victim while others identified her as apocryphal but still searched for a case to account for her invention.

Robertson was obviously a writer who was not going to let his lack of information spoil a good story. He 'knew' that there must have been a murder in December 1887, as the press reports of the later Whitechapel murders referred to it. The fact that he couldn't find a report of it didn't matter, so he resorted to building his story from other sources, and his piece contains echoes of the murders of both Emma Smith and Catherine Eddowes. A phrase in his opening section holds the vital clue: 'The "Ripper's" story needs no trimmings. There is horror by the bucketful in the dour police and medical evidence of the time. In this report I have stuck to the official records as far as possible and have quoted from eye-witness accounts chronicled in the columns of Reynolds News'.

How to explain the mysterious murder of December 1887? Many have speculated that it was press confusion over the date of the murder of Emma Smith, and in some ways this is correct. *Lloyd's Weekly Newspaper* carried a report on the inquest into the murder of Emma Smith. In this report is the following crucial passage:

> Another woman gave evidence that she had last seen Emma Smith between 12 and 1 on Tuesday morning, talking to a man in a black dress [sic], wearing a white neckerchief. It was near Farrant-street, Burdett-road. She was hurrying away from the neighbourhood, as she had herself been struck in the mouth a few minutes before by some young men. She did not believe that the man talking to Smith was one of them. The quarter was a fearfully rough one. Just before Christmas last she had been injured by men under circumstances of a similar nature, and was a fortnight in the infirmary [authors' emphasis].[5]

Here is a serious attack on a woman in the right area and at the right time to account for the story of a murder around Christmas of 1887. Indeed, the attack was so serious that she was detained in the infirmary for three weeks, and the story of this attack was told at the inquest into Emma Smith's murder, thus providing a press source. The victim of the December 1887 attack was Margaret Hames, a widow aged fifty-four, of the same address as Emma Smith, who was admitted to the Whitechapel infirmary on 8 December 1887, with chest and face injuries. She was not released until two days after Boxing Day.[6] It can be seen, then, that the unknown victim (later named 'Fairy Fay') was born of the Christmas Week 1887 attack on Margaret Hames, a few months before the murder of Emma Smith, which was the first of the series of Whitechapel murders.

CHAPTER FOUR

Murder in George Yard

'The case would be left in the hands of Detective-inspector Reid, who would endeavour to discover the perpetrator of this dreadful murder.'

The Times

In 1888 both the East End and the C.I.D. were in a state of flux. The population of the East End was about 600,000 and included the poorest areas of the capital. It was an area with high immigration and itinerant workers, which included large market and dock areas. There were large numbers of common lodging houses in the area and a very high prostitution rate. For many women—and men for that matter—prostitution and theft were the sole sources of income. By August 1888 there had been several changes at Scotland Yard. In charge at Central Office C.I.D. was the much respected Chief Constable Adolphus Williamson, a career police officer who at this time was a sick man with heart disease (he died in 1889). Replacing him as superintendent was John Shore, another experienced career officer who was kept busy in the office running the whole department. Under him at Scotland Yard were five chief inspectors—Greenham, Neame, Butcher, Littlechild, and Swanson—and fourteen inspectors. Overall head of the C.I.D. was James Monro, who did not get on with the chief commissioner, Sir Charles Warren. Monro wanted sole control of the C.I.D., whilst Warren wanted overall control of all departments. This led to Monro's resignation in August 1888 and his replacement by Dr Robert Anderson. Anderson, a barrister working in the Prison Department, was quickly appointed to succeed him, taking up the position of junior assistant commissioner on the day of Nichols' murder. On the same day Alexander Carmichael Bruce took up the post of senior assistant commissioner of police. [1]

Emma Smith's murder was all but forgotten when a second prostitute murder occurred on 7 August 1888, a bank holiday. This time the body of Martha Tabram (or Turner) was found at 4.45 a.m. by a resident, John Reeves, on the first floor landing of George Yard Buildings, George Yard, Whitechapel, a tenement block. She had been stabbed thirty-nine times, apparently with two different weapons. Most of the stabs appeared to have been inflicted with a penknife, whilst one, which had penetrated the sternum, appeared to have been made by a much stronger, dagger-like weapon, or, possibly, a sword bayonet. Again Reid took charge of the case. It was a brutal attack. The murder was believed to have occurred around 2.30 a.m. and Tabram had last been seen in the company of a soldier at 12.45 a.m., going up George Yard, by a friend, 'Pearly Poll' Connolly, another prostitute. Also the beat policeman, PC Barrett, had spoken with a soldier at 2.00 a.m. at the end of George Yard at its junction with Wentworth Street, and he had stated that he was waiting for a 'chum' who had 'gone off with a girl'.

Inspector Reid and PC Barratt went to the Tower of London Barracks which was within the H Division boundary, where the Sergeant Major took Barrett to the guardroom and he was shown several prisoners. Barrett was unable to identify anyone, saying that he couldn't because they were not dressed in uniform. Reid arranged a parade of all the corporals and privates who had been on leave on the 6th. He warned PC Barrett to 'be careful as to his actions because many eyes were watching him and a great deal depended on his picking the right man and no other.' This could have done little for the unfortunate Barrett's confidence. When the parade had assembled Reid instructed Barrett to 'walk along the rank and touch the man if he was there.' Reid and the officers from the barracks stood back to observe Barrett, who moved along the rank 'from left to right until he reached about the centre when he stepped up to a private wearing medals and touched him.' Barrett then approached Reid and told him that he had picked out the man. Reid told him to be certain and to have another look, upon which Barrett did so and promptly passed along the rank, picking out a second man about six or seven away from the first. One can only imagine that Reid's prompting had unnerved Barrett, and Reid asked him how he came to pick out two. Barrett replied, 'The man I saw in George Yard had no medals and the first man I picked out had.' Reid directed Barrett to stand away. The two men picked out by Barrett were taken to the orderly room, but the man wearing medals was allowed to go when Barrett stated that he had made a mistake. The other gave the name of John Leary. Reid questioned Leary as to his movements on the Monday night, and he said that he had been in Brixton with a Private Law until the pubs closed. Reid concluded that 'the PC had made a great mistake and I allowed the man to leave the orderly room.'

Two other witnesses, Jane Gillbank and her daughter, had seen Tabram with a private of the Guards on the Sunday before her murder. Detective Sergeants Leach and Caunter took them to the barracks, but they failed to pick out the soldier they had seen. Reid returned to the barracks to await the return of Corporal Benjamin, who had been absent without leave since 6 August. He eventually returned to the barracks at 11 p.m. and Reid 'at once took charge of his clothing and bayonet, and asked him to account for his time.' The corporal was able to account for his time and nothing incriminating was found.

Reid had arranged for Tabram's friend Connolly to attend a parade at the barracks at 11 a.m. on 11 August. She failed to turn up and could not be found. Sergeant Caunter tracked her down on the 12th and she attended a parade at the Tower at 11 a.m. on the 13th. Upon seeing the line-up she stated, 'They are not here, they had white bands round their caps.' This indicated that they were seeking members of the Coldstream Guards, not the Scots Guards.

Thus the process was repeated at Wellington Barracks, where the Coldstreams were quartered. Reid noted that 'she picked out two privates as the men who were with her and the deceased on the night of the murder.' She said that she was 'quite positive [they] were the men who had been with her and her companion.' However, the two men—George, who was the one who had remained with her, and Skipper, who had been Tabram's client—proved an alibi and the identification failed. Reid had to admit defeat with the attempted identifications. The police failed to find any other witnesses who had seen Tabram and Pearly Poll with the soldiers on the night of the murder. Neither PC Barrett or Connolly could be used as witnesses again for having picked out the wrong men, 'they could not be trusted again and their evidence would be worthless.'

Between the two identification parades Reid, wearing his smart blue serge suit, had attended Tabram's inquest, which was held at the Working Lads' Institute in Whitechapel Road. The press noted that Reid sat through the hearing 'without taking so much as a note' and that he 'seemed to be absorbing all the material points.' The inquest was adjourned.[2]

Thursday 23 August, the final day of the inquest, saw Reid arrive at the Working Lads' Institute at around 1.30 p.m. Reid sat to the right of the coroner. He was again wearing his blue serge coat and waistcoat but now with light striped trousers. Reid crossed his legs 'and stared blankly at the assembled jurymen.'[3] When Connolly was called to give evidence Reid asked that she might be cautioned, so the deputy coroner, George Collier, 'explained that she need not answer any question, but what she did say would be taken down and could be used in evidence against her on a future occasion.'[4] Connolly stated that she had 'left the corporal at the corner of George Yard about 5 or 10 minutes past 12, and afterwards went along Commercial Street towards Whitechapel. She heard no screams and was first informed of the murder on the Tuesday.'

'Did you threaten to drown yourself since this occurrence?' Reid asked Connolly.

'Yes, but only in a lark,' she replied. 'I went to my cousin's and stayed there for two days. My cousin lives in Fuller's Court, Drury Lane.'

It was Reid's opinion that after learning of Tabram's murder, Connolly 'kept out of the way purposely, and it was only by searching that they found her.' As the inquest drew to a close Reid 'informed the court that many persons had come forward and made statements which, when threshed out, ended unsatisfactorily, and up to the present the police had been unable to secure the guilty party or parties.'

The verdict of 'wilful murder by person or persons unknown' was inevitably returned, and Reid concluded his report by saying that he 'informed the court that careful inquiries are still being made with a view to obtain information regarding the case.'[5] The crime remained undetected. In fairness to Reid, he had done as much as he could; these sorts of crimes, involving prostitutes, are always the most difficult to detect. Often the offenders are not known to the victims, whose own lifestyles and dislike of the police did not help matters. There was much worse to come.

CHAPTER FIVE

The Whitechapel Murders

'People afar off smelled blood, and the superstitious said that the skies were of a deeper red that autumn.'

Famous Crimes Past and Present – Harold Furniss

A third murder took place in the early hours of Friday 31 August 1888, in Buck's Row, Whitechapel. The victim was yet another prostitute, Mary Ann 'Polly' Nichols, aged forty-five, of lodgings at 18 Thrawl Street, Spitalfields. Despite the location, the scene of the murder actually fell under the aegis of Reid's old division, J or Bethnal Green, the local inspector then being Joseph Helson. Nichols' body was found about 3.45 a.m. by a carman, Charles Cross, who was shortly joined by a second, Robert Paul, both of whom were on their way to work. After they went off to find a police officer, the local beat officer, PC 97J Neil, discovered the body. Dr Llewellyn was called out and declared that Nichols' throat had been savagely slashed but noticed no other mutilation. The night duty uniformed inspector was John Spratling and it was he who later found that Nichols's abdomen had been opened with two jagged cuts and minor stab wounds inflicted on the genitals; Dr Llewellyn was again called out. Spratling and Detective Sergeant George Godley searched the vicinity of the murder. The brutal nature of the murder was a sensation for the press, who immediately linked all three murders and declared that a maniac was at large in the area.

Robbery was ruled out as a motive, and the police conducted house-to-house enquiries and a search of the area. Local Inspector Joseph Helson initially conducted the inquiry, but Scotland Yard was called in immediately, as both police and press realised the seriousness of the attack and the possibility that the murder was part of a series. Three inspectors were sent in by the Yard to conduct the investigation, inspectors Abberline, Henry Moore and Walter Andrews. As an inspector first-class, Abberline was the senior man, and he directed the investigation assisted by his own men and the local C.I.D. Placed in overall charge of the case, by Commissioner Warren, with his office at Scotland Yard, was Chief Inspector Donald Sutherland Swanson. It had, apparently, at last become too big for the local C.I.D. alone to manage.

Suspicion was attached to three local slaughtermen, Tomkins, Britton, and Mumford, but they were absolved after questioning. The inquiries were summed up in a report by Swanson, who concluded 'the absence of motive which leads to violence and of any scrap of evidence direct or circumstantial, left the police without the slightest shadow of a trace.

The time may not have been propitious, but at the end of the first week of September the new head of the C.I.D., Dr Robert Anderson, went on sick leave, under doctor's orders, to Switzerland.[1] On the morning of Saturday 8 September 1888, another prostitute died. This time the killing took place in the rear yard of 29 Hanbury Street, Spitalfields, just around the corner from Commercial Street Police Station. The victim was Annie Chapman, forty-seven years old, a resident of Crossingham's common lodging house at 35 Dorset Street, Spitalfields. This time the mutilation was even more horrendous. Chapman was found dead about 6.00 a.m. by one of the occupants of No. 29, John Davies. There were signs of strangulation and her throat had been deeply cut back to the vertebrae. She had been opened up and disembowelled; part of her intestines were draped over her left shoulder, and her uterus and its appendages, with the upper portion of the vagina and the posterior two-thirds of the bladder, had been removed and taken away. In the absence of Reid, who was on annual leave, the inquiry was started by Inspector Joseph Chandler of H Division, who was the first police officer on the scene; he liaised with the doctor in attendance, police surgeon Dr Bagster Phillips, who arrived at 6.30 a.m. Two brass rings—a wedding and a keeper—had been wrenched from Chapman's finger and had been taken away by the killer. A small piece of coarse muslin, a small-tooth comb, and a pocket comb in a paper case were found near her feet. These items 'had apparently been placed there in order—that is to say arranged there,' stated the doctor. Also found in the yard were two pills contained in a portion of envelope bearing a Sussex Regiment seal in blue and a red postmark, 'London,

Aug. 23, 1888'. On this piece of envelope were the handwritten letters 'M' and (lower down) 'Sp', as well as (apparently at the commencement of the address) the figure '2'. This was initially treated as a clue, but inquiries revealed that it had belonged to Chapman and was not a clue to the identity of her assailant.

Dr Phillips gave 'it as his opinion that the murderer was possessed of anatomical knowledge from the manner of the removal of viscera, & that the knife used was not an ordinary knife, but such as a small amputating knife, or a well ground slaughterman's knife, narrow & thin, sharp & blade of six to eight inches in length.' These proved to be significant words as they appeared to establish that the killer had some medical knowledge and so may be a medical man. The police again searched the lodging houses for any suspicious or bloodstained lodgers who had returned on the morning of the murder, as well as pawnbrokers' shops for the two missing rings. The rings were never located. Police inquiries were again headed by Inspector Abberline.

It emerged that Chapman had been last seen alive at 2.00 a.m. by Timothy Donovan, the deputy of the lodging house at 35 Dorset Street when she was under the influence of drink and had no money to pay for a bed. She thus left the lodging house and walked into the dark streets of Spitalfields. At 4.45 a.m. John Richardson of 2 John Street, Spitalfields, the son of Mrs Amelia Richardson who lived at 29 Hanbury Street, went to No. 29 to check the security of the cellar door in the backyard. At that time he sat on the rear steps of the house and cut a piece of leather from one of his boots. It was still dark but light enough in this pre-dawn period to see the entire yard. He saw no body. At 5.25 a.m. Albert Cadosch of the neighbouring No. 27 went into his backyard and although it was separated from 29 by a wooden fence, preventing him from seeing next door, he heard people talking and made out the word 'No'. Cadosch went back indoors but again returned to the yard at 5.28 a.m. These times sound very exact for an age when timekeeping was hardly accurate. This time he heard a noise in the yard of No. 29 'as of something falling against the fence.' Although by now it was light he took no further notice nor did he attempt to look into the adjacent yard.

At about 5.30 a.m., around the time of Chapman's death, another witness had seen a woman standing outside 29 Hanbury Street in conversation with a man. It was daylight and the witness, Mrs Elizabeth Long, also known as Durrell,[2] identified Chapman upon viewing her body. She stated that the man had been standing facing Chapman with his back to the witness, who approached from the direction of Brick Lane. Mrs Long heard the man say, 'Will you?' and Chapman had replied, 'Yes'. Elizabeth Long passed by on the same footpath, taking no further note of the couple. She described the man as 'apparently over 40 years of age'; she did not see his full face but he appeared to be dark, 'he appeared to be a little taller than the woman and looked like a foreigner.' Mrs Long also believed that he was wearing a dark coat and a brown deerstalker hat. He was of 'shabby-genteel' appearance. The evidence of other witnesses seemed to confirm the time of death as being around 5.30 a.m., so this is probably one of the best witness descriptions of the killer. Long did not think that she could identify the man if she saw him again, however, as she had not seen his face.

The murders of Nichols and Chapman would certainly appear to have been committed by the same hand, and further mutilation in the case of Nichols was possibly prevented by the approach of the witness Cross causing the killer to flee before carrying out his intentions. This latest killing was confirmation, as far as police, press, and public were concerned, that an unknown, silent, and cunning maniac was at large. The scene was set, and the scene was the 'manor' of Detective Inspector Reid.

CHAPTER SIX

Hunting the Maniac

'You always were a very keen investigator – a d——n sight too keen sometimes.'

H.L. Adam to Edmund Reid

Whether or not popular opinion was correct, the public imagination had been fired, press interest had been kindled and the police had problems. Reid returned from his leave into the cauldron that was the East End of September 1888. Without a doubt the C.I.D. did not lack experienced and resourceful men at the 'sharp end' of things. At the top, however, it was a little different, and the nature of the leadership of such a body, as well as its problems, permeated the whole.

The long-standing acrimony between the head of the C.I.D., Assistant Commissioner James Monro, and the Chief Commissioner, Sir Charles Warren, had come to a head, for the two men found it impossible to work efficiently together. As we have already seen, the trouble was that Monro wanted autonomy over his detective force and Warren wanted control of the whole of the Metropolitan Police. The petty bickering and machinations of Monro behind Warren's back, neither man being faultless, resulted in a reduction of the efficiency of the detective force at this critical time. The situation could not last. Near the end of August Monro finally resigned his post, leaving the C.I.D. without a leader.

The appointment of Anderson, however, did not resolve the immediate problem. After a week of familiarising himself with his new office at Scotland Yard, Anderson went off on his month's holiday to Switzerland. He was, he claimed, suffering from the stress of his work and the leave was taken on his doctor's orders. He left on the day before Chapman's murder, effectively leaving the detectives without their leader. The seriousness of the emerging terror in the East End was, perhaps, not as apparent when Anderson left as it was shortly to become. It was a gift for the critical press and a problem for the Home Office. Extant reports show that in the absence of Anderson, Senior Assistant Commissioner Alexander Carmichael Bruce performed office duties in his stead. Under Bruce was the hugely experienced but very sick Chief Constable Adolphus 'Dolly' Williamson, then Superintendent John Shore, followed by the Chief Inspectors and Inspectors.

Sir Charles Warren was distressed and annoyed by Anderson's absence, for he needed a man to take the helm in this important matter. A report of 15 September 1888, from Warren to the Assistant Commissioner C.I.D., stated:

> I am convinced that the Whitechapel murder case is one which can be successfully grappled with if it is systematically taken in hand. I go so far as to say that I could myself in a few days unravel the mystery provided I could spare the time & give individual attention to it. I feel therefore the utmost importance to be attached to putting the whole Central Office work in this case in the hands of one man who will have nothing else to concern himself with. Neither you or I or Mr. Williamson can do this, I therefore put it in the hands of Chief Inspr. Swanson who must be acquainted with <u>every detail</u>.

Thus Warren designated one man, with his own office at the Yard, to take full control of the Whitechapel inquiry. He was to see every piece of paper regarding the case before action was taken, unless urgency dictated otherwise. The report appears to be in the hand of an amanuensis, with a footnote in Warren's own hand at the end, presumably added to reinforce his instructions:

> Every document, letter received, or telegram on this subject should go to his room before being dictated, & he should be responsible for its being dictated when necessary. This is [to] avoid the possibility of documents being delayed or action retarded.
> CW 15.9.88[1]

The instruction was sent the same day to Assistant Commissioner Bruce and was seen and noted by Shore and Williamson before going to Swanson. Thus the leadership of the inquiry team was established in the absence of Anderson. The case was now high profile and the Home Office was uneasy about the situation at the top of the C.I.D. and their apparent lack of success. In a memo to his Principal Private Secretary, Evelyn Ruggles-Brise, Home Secretary Henry Matthews wrote on 22 September 1888: 'Stimulate the Police about Whitechapel murders. *Absente* Anderson, Monro might be willing to give a hint to the C.I.D. people if needful.'[2]

This pointed remark indicated that Matthews felt the C.I.D. lacked the direction it needed and that, perhaps, the old chief could be called upon to assist in giving some help. Anderson's absence was not sitting easily with his masters and the newspapers were commenting on it. A suggestion to search the houses in the locality was made in a letter from Sir W. Ellis, MP, and was commented upon by Warren in a letter dated 4 October 1888, forwarding it to the Home Office. Matthews replied, stating (*inter alia*) that

I thought my own suggestion of last Wed. more practical—take all houses in a given area which appear suspicious upon the best inquiry your detectives can make. Search all those, which the owners or persons in charge will allow you to search. Where leave is refused, apply to a magistrate for a search warrant, on the ground that it is probable or possible the murderer may be there. If search warrants are refused, you can only keep the houses under observation. I shd. be glad now that the week is closing of a report of all the measures that have been taken for arresting the criminal, & of the results—Have any of the doctors examined the eyes of the murdered woman.

A postscript pointedly added: 'I shall be very glad to hear whether Mr. Anderson's health has permitted him to resume his duties.' The increasing concern was conveyed to Anderson, who noted in his memoirs:

And letters from Whitehall decided me to spend the last week of my holiday in Paris, that I might be in touch with my office. On the night of my arrival in the French capital two more victims fell to the knife of the murder fiend; and next day's post brought me an urgent appeal from Mr. Matthews to return to London, and of course I complied.[3]

CHAPTER SEVEN

Suspects

'The names bring back memories of terrible crimes and tragedies.'
Edmund Reid

The police were interested in several suspects believed to have anatomical knowledge and a disturbed state of mind. Three 'medical students' came to the fore. Two were quickly found and eliminated from the inquiry. The third, John Sanders, proved more elusive. Sanders was the son of an Indian Army surgeon and had himself undertaken training at the London Medical Hospital in 1879. He later became insane and violent, attacking his friends. His last known address, Aberdeen Place, St Johns Wood, was checked. All that could be established was that a woman named Sanders had lived at No. 20 but had gone abroad about two years previously. John Sanders, in fact, was a patient at West Malling Place, a private asylum in Kent, at the time of the murders. He died in a lunatic asylum in Exeter in 1902, aged thirty-seven.

Oswald Puckridge, who had been released from an asylum on 4 August, came under scrutiny. He was trained as a surgeon and had allegedly 'threatened to rip people up with a long knife.' Puckridge was fifty in 1888 and died in a workhouse in 1900. There is no record of his final status as a suspect.

Swiss butcher Joseph (Jacob) Isenschmid, a former patient at Colney Hatch asylum, where he had spent ten weeks in 1887 before discharge, became the first significant suspect. He had left his wife of twenty-one years around July of 1888, taking two butcher's knives with him. When interviewed Mrs Isenschmid stated that she thought her husband was only dangerous to her, adding, 'I think he would kill me if he had the chance. He is fond of other women. He is known as the mad butcher.' His new landlord, Mr Tyler, noted that he kept irregular hours and was frequently out in the early hours. The police felt that he 'was not unlikely to have been the person engaged in committing the recent murders in Whitechapel' and put his house under observation. He was arrested on 12 September and then taken to Bow asylum. Abberline was cautiously optimistic, saying that 'at present we are unable to procure any evidence to convict him with the murders. He appears to be the most likely person that has come under our notice to have committed the crimes, and every effort will be made to account for his movements on dates in question.' Isenschmid was eventually eliminated from the inquiry.

William Piggott, formerly an affluent publican but by 1888 a ship's cook, was arrested in Gravesend. He had walked into a pub and spoke of his hatred of women. A woman had bitten his hand in Whitechapel and injured it. Additionally he had left a parcel in a fish shop, which on examination was found to contain a bloodstained shirt. Abberline brought him back to London, but he was able to account for himself at the times of the murders.

Charles Ludwig, a forty-year-old German hairdresser, was arrested on 18 September after scaring a prostitute by pulling a long knife on her, then later drunkenly threatening a bystander with his knife at a coffee stall. When searched at the police station he was found to be in possession of a long-bladed clasp knife, a razor, and a pair of scissors. Police inquiries revealed that Ludwig had gained medical knowledge in the German Army and used the services of prostitutes. The day after Chapman's murder he had turned up at a hotel with a case of razors and a pair of scissors. His hands were bloodstained and he talked of the murders. He too was eliminated from any suspicion of guilt.

Another high-profile and most promising suspect of this time was John Pizer, known as 'Leather Apron'. Police questioning of prostitutes after the Nichols murder revealed 'that a feeling of terror existed against a man known as Leather Apron who it appears has for a considerable time been levying blackmail and ill-using them if his demands were not complied with although there is no evidence to connect him with the murder.' The police obviously felt that this man needed to answer some questions and they immediately sought him out.

The press reported:

From all accounts he is five feet four or five inches in height and wears a dark, close-fitting cap. He is thickset, and has an unusually thick neck. His hair is black, and closely clipped, his age being about 38 or 40. He has a small, black moustache. The distinguishing feature of his costume is a leather apron which he always wears, and from which he gets his nickname. His expression is sinister, and seems to be full of terror for the women who describe it. His eyes are small and glittering. His lips are usually parted in a grin which is not only not reassuring, but excessively repellent.[1]

Detective Sergeant William Thick arrested this epitome of evil on Monday 10 September 1888 at 22 Mulberry Street, off Commercial Road East. The keeper of the lodging house where he had stayed corroborated his alibi for the night of Nichols' murder. On the night of Chapman's murder he had stayed with relatives. Abberline concluded that 'the suspicions were groundless.'

By now the case was achieving international notoriety, and the German police at Bremen offered up a suspect, a male barber known as 'Mary'. He had been arrested for sticking sharp instruments into women's breasts, but it was later found that he was imprisoned at Osterhausen on the relevant dates. With Ludwig and Isenschmid still detained, two further murders occurred.

CHAPTER EIGHT

Double Atrocity

> 'Even now I can recall the foggy evenings, and hear again the raucous cries of the newspaper boys: "Another horrible murder, murder, mutilation, Whitechapel."'
>
> Melville Macnaghten

At 12.45 a.m. on Sunday 30 September 1888, a non-English-speaking Hungarian Jew named Israel Schwartz, was making his way along Berner Street, St. George's-in-the-East, from the direction of Commercial Road. He went into Leman Street Police Station late Sunday afternoon with the following story: '[I] saw a man stop & speak to a woman, who was standing in the gateway.' The gateway was that leading into Dutfield's Yard and giving access to the International Working Men's Educational Club, where there was a late-night singsong going on following a meeting. Schwartz watched as

> The man tried to pull the woman into the street, but he turned her round & threw her down on the footway & the woman screamed three times, but not very loudly. On crossing to the opposite side of the street, he saw a second man standing lighting his pipe. The man who threw the woman down called out apparently to the man on the opposite side of the road 'Lipski' & then Schwartz walked away, but finding that he was followed by the second man he ran as far as the railway arch but the man did not follow so far.

The woman attacked was later identified by Schwartz as Elizabeth Stride, a prostitute, whose body was found lying just inside the gates of Dutfield's Yard at 1.00 a.m. by the returning club steward, Louis Diemschütz, who had been out with his costermonger's barrow and pony the previous day hawking cheap jewellery. Her throat had been cut, but there was no other mutilation to her body. This spot, on a fairly busy street outside a social club that was in session, did not seem the typical, out-of-the-way site as with the previous victims. Indeed, an attack on the woman had been witnessed by at least two persons, and unless the unlikely circumstance that the woman was attacked twice in the same location in fifteen minutes had occurred, the man seen by Schwartz was her murderer. Schwartz had seen the man stop and speak to the woman, followed immediately by an attack on her. Thus the indications are that the man had immediately approached and attacked the woman without preliminaries, possibly indicating that he knew her and that the assault was the continuation of some sort of dispute with her. In other words, the likelihood would seem to be that Stride and her attacker knew each other.

Schwartz described the woman's attacker as aged about thirty years, five feet five inches tall, fair complexion, dark hair, small brown moustache, full face, broad-shouldered, and dressed in dark jacket and trousers, black cap with a peak, and was carrying nothing. The man with the pipe he described as aged thirty-five years, five feet eleven inches tall, fresh complexion, light brown hair, brown moustache, and dressed in a dark overcoat, an old black hard felt hat with a wide brim, and with a clay pipe in his hand. Inspector Abberline questioned Schwartz closely on the Sunday evening and the police felt that his story was the truth. A house-to-house inquiry was made in Berner Street and the neighbourhood, but no suspect was located. With regard to Schwartz the police referred to his evidence being given at the inquest, but no record of this was carried in the newspaper reports. A possible answer to this apparent mystery is the fact that Schwartz did not speak English; the coroner, therefore, without verbal testimony being given, accepted his written statement. The rules for evidence at coroners' inquests have a much greater breadth and laxity than those pertaining in a normal court of law. As regards the shout of 'Lipski', a probable explanation was given by Inspector Abberline, who stated that the name had been used as a derogatory address to Jews since the execution the previous year of the Jew Israel Lipski for the poisoning of Miriam Angel in nearby Batty Street.

The *Star* carried Schwartz' story with some odd variations. The reporter used an interpreter to obtain his story:

It seems that he had gone out for the day, and his wife had expected to move, during his absence, from their lodgings in Berner-street to others in Backchurch-lane. When he came homewards about a quarter before one he first walked down Berner-street to see if his wife had moved. As he turned the corner from Commercial-road he noticed some distance in front of him a man walking as if partially intoxicated. He walked on behind him, and presently he noticed a woman standing in the entrance to the alley way where the body was afterwards found. The half-tipsy man halted and spoke to her. The Hungarian saw him put his hand on her shoulder and push her back into the passage, but, feeling rather timid of getting mixed up in quarrels, he crossed to the other side of the street. Before he had gone many yards, however, he heard the sound of a quarrel and turned back to learn what was the matter, but just as he stepped from the kerb a second man came out of the doorway of the public-house a few doors off, and shouting out some sort of warning to the man who was with the woman, rushed forwards as if to attack the intruder. The Hungarian states positively that he saw a knife in this second man's hand but he waited to see no more. He fled incontinently, to his new lodgings. He described the man with the woman as about 30 years of age, rather stoutly built, and wearing a brown moustache. He was dressed respectably in dark clothes and felt hat. The man who came at him with a knife he also describes, but not in detail. He says he was taller than the other, but not so stout, and that his moustaches were red. Both men seemed to belong to the same grade of society. The police have arrested one man answering the description the Hungarian furnished. This prisoner has not been charged, but is held for inquiries to be made. The truth of the man's statement is not wholly accepted.[1]

This account is so different from the one obtained by the police that it would seem to indicate that there was a difference in the quality of the translation made by each interpreter. The question is whose was the most accurate, the one used by the police or the one used by the reporter? In the final analysis it has to be said that the official one must be preferred over that given by the press.

The following day the *Star* ran another story on Schwartz, which does little to dispel the mystery:

In the matter of the Hungarian who said he saw a struggle between a man and a woman in the passage where the Stride body was afterwards found, the Leman-street police have reason to doubt the truth of the story. They arrested one man on the description thus obtained, and a second on that furnished from another source, but they are not likely to act further on the same information without additional facts.[2]

Inspector Reid was at the Commercial Street Police Office that Sunday morning at 1.25 a.m. when he received a telegram notifying him of the murder, and he at once attended the scene. He conferred with the other police officers and doctors at the scene, and a search was made without result. All persons in the yard as well as club members, twenty-eight of them, were searched and their details obtained before being allowed to go. The houses abutting the yard were checked, occupants' details taken and a search made. They even forced the door of a loft, which locked on the inside, but without result. Reid 'minutely examined the wall near where the body was found but could find no spots of blood.' The body was removed to the mortuary at 4.30 a.m.; Reid went to the coroner's residence and informed him of the death personally. He then returned to the yard and, meticulous as ever, made another search, as it was then daylight and checked the walls in the yard thoroughly but could find no sign of them having been recently scaled. Reid then went to the mortuary and took down a full description of the body and clothing. He then circulated the description:

I guessed her age as 42, length 5 ft 2 in, complexion pale, hair dark brown and curly. I raised an eyelid and found that her eyes were light grey; I parted her lips and found that she had lost her upper teeth in front. She had on an old black jacket trimmed with fur. Fastened on the right side was a small bunch of flowers, consisting of maidenhair fern and a red rose. She had two light serge petticoats, white stockings, white chemise with insertion in front, side-spring boots, and black crape bonnet. In her jacket pocket I found two pocket handkerchiefs, a thimble, and a piece of wool on a card.[3]

A press report detailed the sort of information that Reid was receiving from the local prostitutes and the difficulties it presented:

Detective Inspector Reid who has charge of the case, had a great deal of information volunteered to him by women of the class to which the victim belonged regarding men whom they allege to have threatened them with death. Each informant is convinced that the man she saw was the unknown who is now so keenly searched for, but as the description varies in each case it is quite plain that they cannot refer to the same person. According to one he is a thick set and close shaven man, with a short coat and dark trousers; another states that he is a pretty tall man, with short dark whiskers and a beard; a third speaks of him as shortish with light whiskers; sometimes he wears a dark ulster, and at others a checked one; now he is well dressed, and again shabby genteel; and altogether the descriptions given are so confusing that they afford no guide to any officer. It would seem that in Whitechapel, Stepney, and Spitalfields there are several petty ruffians who level blackmail upon these women under threats of mutilation, and, after parting with any sum they may possess, the wretched females tell either a constable or some of their neighbours that they have had a narrow escape from the murderer, and give a description of him.[4]

The lengthy Stride inquest began on Monday 1 October 1888 at the Vestry Hall, Cable Street, St George's-in-the-East. Reid attended on behalf of the C.I.D. Reid himself gave evidence and was questioned by the coroner, Wynne Baxter:

Baxter: All the people who came into the yard were detained and searched?
Reid: Yes, and their names and addresses were taken. The first question was whether they had any knives. They were then asked to account for their presence there.
A Juror: It would have been possible for anyone to have escaped from the yard if he had been hiding there while you went into the club to inform the members?
Reid: Yes, it would have been possible; but as soon as I informed the members every one went out, and I do not think it would have been possible for anyone to get out then.
A Juror: If anyone had run up the yard, you would have seen him?
Reid: Yes, because it is dark just in the gateway; but further up the yard you could see anybody running or walking by the lights of the club.
A Juror: Do you think that anyone could have come out of the gateway without you seeing them?
Reid: No, I think they could not.

Wynne Baxter addressed the question of the victim's identity:

Baxter: Is the body identified yet?
Reid: Not yet.

Foreman: I cannot understand that, as she is called Elizabeth Stride.

Baxter: That has not yet been sworn to, but something is known of her. It is known where she lived. You had better leave that point until tomorrow.

The following day, at the resumed inquest, Reid questioned PC Lamb as to his beat on the night of the murder and explained that there were also fixed-point constables on duty, 'so if a person wanted a constable he would not have to go all the way to the station for one.' On Wednesday's sitting Reid asked Elizabeth Tanner, deputy of the common lodging house at 32 Flower and Dean Street, 'Have you ever heard the name of Stride mentioned in connection with her?' Tanner had not.

Michael Kidney, Stride's lover, proved to be an awkward witness:

Kidney: On Monday night I went to Leman Street police station for a detective to act on my information, but I could not get one.

Reid: Were you intoxicated?

Kidney: Yes.

Baxter: It is not too late yet; can you give us any information now?

Kidney: I have heard something said that leads me to believe that had I been able to act the same as a detective I could have got a lot more information. I asked for a young detective. I told the inspector at the station that if the murder occurred on my beat I would shoot myself. I have been in the army.

Reid: Will you give me any information now?

Kidney: I believe I could catch the man, if I had the proper force at my command. If I was to place the men myself I could capture the murderer. He would be caught in the act.

Reid: Then you have no information to give?

Kidney: No.

Reid testified on the Friday, giving details of his actions on the night of the murder, and concluded that 'the police engaged in the inquiry had made house to house inquiry in the immediate neighbourhood, with the result that we have been able to produce the witnesses which have appeared before you. The inquiry is still going on. Every endeavour is being made to arrest the assassin, but up to the present without success.'

The question of Stride's correct identity was resolved by Reid at the final sitting of the inquest on Tuesday 23 October 1888:

> since the last sitting I have made inquiries and examined the books of the Sick Asylum, Bromley, and found therein an entry of the death of John Thomas Stride, carpenter, of Poplar, on the 24th October, 1884. The nephew of Stride is here to give evidence. I have also seen Elizabeth Watts whose sister is married and resides at Tottenham. She informed me that the whole of Mrs Malcolm's statement is false [Mrs Malcolm had mistakenly thought that the victim was her sister], that she had not seen her sister for years, and believed her to be dead. It was not true that she saw her sister on the Monday before the murder. I have directed her to appear here as a witness today, and she promised to attend.

Baxter expressed regret that such a long inquiry had not led to the arrest of the murderer, but was 'bound to acknowledge the great attention which Inspector Reid and the police had given to the case.' A verdict of wilful murder against some person or persons unknown was returned.[5] In this regard it is interesting to note that the police attached no suspicion to the members of the International Working Men's Institution at 40 Berner Street. Detective Sergeant Patrick McIntyre of the Special Branch later recalled that 'no one believed for a moment that the anonymous stabber was one of their confraternity.'[6]

About the time that Reid was arriving at Berner Street to investigate the Stride murder, another drama was developing in the vicinity of Mitre Square, Aldgate, in the City of London Police area. At 1.35 a.m. three Jews, Joseph Lawende, Joseph Hyam Levy, and Harry Harris, were leaving the Imperial Club, Duke Street, hard by Mitre Square. It had been raining, and they noticed a man and a woman standing talking at the end of Church Passage, which led through into Mitre Square. Only Lawende of the three took any real notice of the two, and that was only a passing look. He was no nearer than about fifteen feet from them and the light was poor, provided only by a nearby gas lamp. The woman had her back to Lawende and her hand was on the man's chest. Levy commented to Harris, 'Look there, I don't like going home by myself when I see those characters about.' The couple appeared to be conversing and the three passed by without so much as a look back. Lawende later said of the man that he 'doubted whether I should know him again,' but described him as aged thirty, five feet seven or eight inches tall, fair complexion, fair moustache, medium build, and wearing a pepper-and-salt coloured loose jacket, a grey cloth cap with a peak of the same colour, a reddish handkerchief tied in a knot around his neck and having the appearance of a sailor. He later identified the woman only by her clothing.

At 1.30 a.m. Police Constable 881 Edward Watkins of the City Police had passed through Mitre Square on his beat, and all was quiet. He returned, entering from Mitre Street, fourteen minutes later. On shining his bull's-eye lantern into the southernmost corner of the Square, he saw the body of a woman lying on her back on the footpath. Her throat was cut, her clothing thrown open, her face mutilated and she had been disembowelled. Watkins called out the night watchman, George Morris, from the nearby Kearley and Tonge warehouse, and assistance was called. The ensuing police activity at last revealed the first real clue. Even as Watkins gazed upon the sad, horrific remains of Catherine Eddowes, her killer was fleeing eastwards away from Mitre Square.

PC 254A Alfred Long had been seconded from his own A (Whitehall) Division to H Division to supplement the strength of his beleaguered colleagues in Whitechapel. At 2.20 a.m. he passed along Goulston Street, only minutes from Mitre Square, and saw nothing. At 2.55 a.m. a return patrol yielded what was to become the only tangible clue in this baffling case. As he shone his bull's-eye lantern into the entrance way to the Model dwellings at 108-119 Goulston Street, he saw lying there a piece of filthy white apron, wet with blood and faeces. It was a portion of Eddowes' apron, which presumably had been cut away by the killer to wipe his soiled hands and knife on and then discarded. On the brick jamb of the doorway above the apron was a message written in chalk: 'The Juwes are The men that Will not be Blamed for nothing.' It was not known if this was written by the killer or not. To the annoyance of the City Police, Sir Charles Warren had the message sponged away at 5.30 a.m., fearing an anti-Jewish uprising. What was certain, at least, was that the killer had fled in an easterly direction from the murder scene, towards the heart of Whitechapel.

Long's evidence of finding the soiled piece of apron and chalked wall message in Goulston Street may not be correct as to timing. He claimed that he had passed the doorway entrance to 108-119 Model Dwellings about 2.20 a.m. on that morning and he stated that the piece of apron was not there then. He further stated that around thirty-five minutes later he was again at the doorway where he discovered the piece of bloodstained apron, and the wall message. This of course leads to the very improbable conclusion that the murderer fled from Mitre Square, at the latest 1.44 a.m., but did not deposit the incriminating piece of apron in the doorway until after 2.20 a.m. As the doorway is only a matter of a few minutes from Mitre Square, we have to ask what would the killer have been doing hanging around the area amid the hue and cry, for at least a full thirty-six minutes? This must throw a question mark over Long's testimony. It is likely that the piece of apron was deposited in the entranceway before 2.00 a.m., as the killer made good his escape. There can be no doubt that those officers engaged on night patrol in the murderer's stamping ground were well briefed as regards the importance checking of all out of the way and ill-lit areas, passageways, entranceways, sheltered areas, etc. in the hunt for the criminal. Even more especially so in the case of an officer such as PC Long who had been specifically drafted in (from A Division) to assist the hard pressed men of H Division. The punitive measures which the Victorian beat policeman was subject to were even highlighted in the press of the day:

> In view of the mystery which surrounds the whereabouts of the murderer or murderers, it might be suggested that the police authorities should take the constables into their confidence, and, for the time being, considering the exceptional circumstances attending the murders, put aside a very stringent rule of the service, the enforcement of which under ordinary condition is absolutely necessary. For instance, it is by no means unusual, doing duty in the streets, to have suspicious incidents come under his observation of which he takes no notice until after he learns of a crime such as has just rekindled public indignation. Under existing circumstances, an officer who made known such 'negligence' would undoubtedly be dismissed the service, and in view of this it cannot be expected that any officer would knowingly bring about his own discharge. Information which might be of the greatest importance as regards a case such as the present is possibly withheld for the very reason that, unless the authorities relax their severity, the man would be bringing about his own downfall.[7]

Probably Long had simply failed to properly check, if indeed he did at all, the doorway at the time that his patrol took him past it at 2.20 a.m., but he could not admit to that. Such an admission could have resulted in a charge of neglect of duty and possible dismissal. Discovery of the piece of apron at the earlier time would have been crucial to any search for, and possible apprehension of, the killer. Much better to simply say that it was not there at the earlier time and it would be very unlikely that such a false statement would be detected. One of the main reasons for the checking of vulnerable premises at night was to detect burglaries, either being committed or freshly committed. It is an unfortunate fact that a policeman would lie when his job (thus his livelihood) was at stake. The grave nature of the Ripper murders, and the importance of carrying out patrol duties correctly, meant that Long, if he wanted to keep his job, simply could not have admitted to failing to check the doorways in Goulston Street properly.

Eddowes' body was conveyed to the mortuary at Golden Lane, as Inspector James McWilliam, chief of the City detective force, and his men began their futile hunt for the killer. Two women had been savagely murdered in one night. Police and press made the obvious assumption: the killer had struck twice inside a single hour. And at this point the killings reached something of a hiatus.

CHAPTER NINE

Jack the Ripper

'The ferocity of a Jack the Ripper . . .'

Winston Churchill

Until this time the unknown killer had largely been referred to in the popular press as 'The Whitechapel Murderer' and 'Leather Apron'. That was now to change. The Central News Agency, operating from offices at 5 New Bridge Street, Ludgate Circus, City, had received a letter dated 25 September 1888, and postmarked 27 September. Written in red ink, in a neat hand, it ran as follows:

Dear Boss, I keep on hearing the police have caught me. but they wont fix me just yet. I have laughed when they look so clever and talk about being on the right track. That joke about Leather Apron gave me real fits. I am down on whores and I shant quit ripping them till I do get buckled. Grand work the last job was, I gave the lady no time to squeal How can they catch me now, I love my work and want to start again. You will soon hear of me with my funny little games. I saved some of the proper red stuff in a ginger beer bottle over the last job to write with but it went thick like glue and I cant use it. Red ink is fit enough I hope ha ha. The next job I do I shall clip the ladys ears off and send to the police officers just for jolly wouldnt you. Keep this letter back till I do a bit more work then give it out straight. My knife's so nice and sharp I want to get to work right away if I get a chance good luck. Yours truly Jack the Ripper Dont mind me giving the trade name.

There was a postscript written at right angles below the signature: 'Wasnt good enough to post this before I got all the red ink off my hands curse it. No luck yet. They say I'm a doctor now ha ha.'

This was a gift for the press, and the name—simple yet incisive—was to ensure the legend. Tom Bulling of the Central News forwarded this letter to Chief Constable Williamson of the C.I.D. on 29 September, stating that the delay had been because they thought it a joke. The letter and name were released to an unsuspecting world on 1 October. Their impact was immediate. An unprecedented flood of hoax mail, most including the words 'Dear Boss' and 'Jack the Ripper', was initiated. Most were simply to be ignored, whilst others were treated more seriously. Indeed, the next communication of significance was a postcard date stamped 1 October. It ran:

I wasn't codding dear old Boss when I gave you the tip. Youll hear about saucy Jacky's work tomorrow double event this time number one squealed a bit couldnt finish straight off. had no time to get ears for police. thanks for keeping last letter back till I got to work again. Jack the Ripper.

On 5 October, Bulling again communicated with Williamson and sent another envelope in the same hand as the first. He wrote out the letter that had been contained in it, which claimed that there would be three victims on the next occasion and was again signed, 'Yours truly Jack the Ripper.' With the panic and publicity caused by this ghoulish turn of events October was to be an eventful month, despite the fact that it was not marked by another murder. The police, it later transpired, were greatly suspicious that Bulling was responsible for the communications in order to enhance copy.[1]

Soon after 6.00 p.m. on Wednesday 3 October 1888, a 32-year-old naval reserve sailor, John Lock, was roaming in the neighbourhood of Ratcliff Highway, allegedly with bloodstains on his coat. A crowd gathered and followed Lock, making threatening comments. He hid in The Victory public house with a man to whom he was known, but the crowd gathered outside the door, shouting 'Leather Apron' and 'Jack the Ripper'. Eventually a policeman arrived and advised Lock to accompany him to the police station and wait there until the crowd had dispersed. Lock was questioned at the King David Place Police Station by the duty inspector while he was waiting in an anteroom. The inspector considered Lock's answers to be quite satisfactory, and after careful scrutiny it was ascertained that the stains on his coat were caused apparently by grease. The noisy crowd had congregated outside the police station but eventually lost interest and dispersed. Lock told the press that the stains were paint.

Lock's story was that he and his wife had been in Australia for several years before coming to England on 28 April. On the day of the incident he had left a friend's house at 85 Balcombe Street, Dorset Square, and made his way to Wapping for the purpose of finding a ship. He met an old acquaintance, which was when he noticed that he was being followed, and they had made their way to the pub. It was claimed that Lock 'had somewhat the appearance of an American.'[2] Lock later wrote to the Home Office, complaining that he had been 'arrested in London on suspicion of being the perpetrator of the Whitechapel murders.'[3]

With the Ripper scare now at its height, the police were receiving much advice and many suggestions relative to the murders. The *Morning Advertiser* gave an example involving Reid himself:

> Inspector Reid has had an interview with a doctor who had suggested that a certain number of women should be paid to walk the streets at night, each of them followed by a plain-clothes detective. The officer pointed out the great risk the women would run, but the doctor suggested that they should wear iron bands round their waists and necks. The plan, however, is regarded by the police as impracticable.[4]

An unpleasant experience in October was to befall the chairman of a public Vigilance Committee set up in Mile End. George Lusk, a well-known local builder, was the leading light of this committee and had received some publicity in the press. He was to receive something rather more unwelcome on the 16th. On that day Lusk found in the post a small parcel, which he unwrapped to disclose a piece of human kidney and a letter written in an untidy scrawl:

> From hell Mr Lusk Sir I send you half the Kidne I took from one women prasarved it for you tother piece I fried and ate it was very nise. I may send you the bloody knif that took it out if you only wate a whil longer. Signed Catch me when you can Mishter Lusk.

The half kidney was examined by the medical men and declared to be human, longitudinally divided. Dr Frederick Gordon Brown, the City Police surgeon, was doubtful that it had belonged to Eddowes. A reporter from the *Sunday Times* had visited Dr Brown while he was examining the piece of kidney. Brown commented:

> So far as I can form an opinion, I do not see any substantial reason why this portion of kidney should not be the portion of the one taken from the murdered woman. I cannot say that it is the left kidney. It must have been cut previously to its being immersed in the spirit which exercised a hardening process. It certainly has not been in spirit for more than a week. As has been stated, there is no portion of the renal artery adhering to it, it having been trimmed up, so, consequently, there could be no correspondence established between the portion of the body from which it was cut. As it exhibits no trace of decomposition, when we consider the length of time that has elapsed since the commission of the murder, we come to the conclusion that the probability is slight of its being a portion of the murdered woman of Mitre-square.[5]

In later years Lusk believed 'that the kidney was sent to him as a practical joke by someone in the London Hospital! This theory of his may of course have been a way of consoling himself for the fright he had when the parcel containing the kidney came to him through the post, he sought police protection for some days after.'[6] The hoaxers, however, if it were they, were having a field day and ensuring the undying notoriety of the unknown murderer.

Dr Brown retained an interest in the Whitechapel murders, attending, at Dr Phillips' invitation, the autopsies on the subsequent victims, and many years later taking members of the Crimes Club (Our Society) around the various sites. All that is known of his conclusions as to the character of the murderer is that 'it could not be due to robbery or jealousy considering the depraved natures of the victims, neither was it for the satisfaction of sexual lust, for in no case had there been violation, but he concluded that it must have been the act of an insane man with full knowledge as a slaughterer and must be classed under the term of Sadism.'[7]

Again numerous suspects were brought to light, but the new batch was altogether less convincing. Greek gypsies proved to have been away from London at the relevant times, and three cowboys from a Wild West show were questioned and eliminated. Dick Austen, a member of the 5th Lancers, was accused by an acquaintance who described him as 'a sharp witty man and a capital scholar.' It was alleged that he hated women and claimed that he would 'kill every whore and cut her inside out.' Abberline failed to locate him.

On Monday 22 October 1888 Annie Hancock, aged thirty-two years, of Brixton stayed out late drinking with several different men. She had been separated from her husband for ten years. At 11.35 p.m. that day she was seen drinking with a stranger in The Northumberland public house. He was described as a tall, fair man with a heavy moustache and brown overcoat. There was no further recorded sighting of her alive. On Friday 9 November her body was pulled out of the Thames off Wapping. The body had been in the water over two weeks and was much discoloured and decomposed. Despite the suspicious circumstances of her death, the coroner's jury later returned an open verdict. It was the discovery of another body the same day, however, that was to attract the attention of the police, press, and public, and ensure that the discovery of poor Annie Hancock passed almost without comment.[8]

Home Secretary, Henry Matthews, was following the events closely and on 22 October 1888 he requested of the Chief Commissioner that 'a report be furnished as to the number both of Brothels and of Common Lodging Houses in Whitechapel, and such information as you may be able to procure as to the numbers and the condition of prostitutes living or plying their calling in the district.'[9]

The reply revealed there were sixty-two houses known to be brothels in the Whitechapel Division, 'and probably a great number of other houses which are more or less intermitently [sic] used for such purposes. The number of Common Lodging Houses is 233, accommodating 8,530 persons.' As to prostitutes, there was no way of making an accurate count, 'but there is an impression that there are about 1,200 prostitutes, mostly of a very low condition.' Matthews further requested, on 25 October, 'a similar report as to the circumstances of the murder in Mitre Square, and of the steps taken in connection therewith so far as the Metropolitan Police are concerned.' Matthews also asked to be furnished with a sketch map showing the position of the scenes of the various murders.[10]

CHAPTER TEN

13 Miller's Court

> 'In my younger days as a detective I did C.I.D. work on a series of crimes much more terrible than the Crippen case. These were the unsolved murders of 'Jack the Ripper.' Compared with Jack the Ripper, Crippen was an angel!'
>
> Chief Inspector Walter Dew.

After the six-week break the terror had diminished, and London was preparing to celebrate the investiture of the new mayor. It was Friday 9 November 1888 and despite the festive mood the landlord of 26 Dorset Street, Spitalfields, John McCarthy, was more concerned with the back rent of 29s owed by one of his tenants, Mary Jane Kelly, at 13 Miller's Court. At 10.45 a.m. he sent his man, Thomas Bowyer, to collect the money. Kelly had been living with Joseph Barnett, an unemployed labourer, for twenty months, the last eight months or so at 13 Miller's Court. She had once told Barnett that she had been to France to live for two weeks but did not like it and so returned. Kelly did, however, like to be called 'Marie Jeanette'. The couple had separated after a disagreement on 30 October, during which dispute a window in the room had been broken.

Bowyer, having had no response to knocking on the door, went to the rear of the ground-floor room, put his hand through the broken window-pane, and pulled aside the material serving as a curtain. He was horrified to see the bloody remains of Kelly on the bed and flesh piled on the bedside table. Her face had been mutilated beyond recognition. Kelly's body had been opened and the contents strewn around the bed, her left hand had been thrust into the thoracic cavity. The inner surfaces of both her thighs had been denuded of flesh to the bone. The door to the room was locked.

The police were summoned by McCarthy, who on arrival at Commercial Street Police Station 'inquired at first for Inspector Reid.'[1] Reid was obviously not available at that time, as McCarthy saw Inspector Walter Beck, the on duty uniform inspector. Beck sent messages to Reid and Abberline,[2] then with Detective Constable Walter Dew hurried to the scene with uniformed officers. Others soon arrived: 'although detectives Thicke [sic], Reid, and a host of others from Scotland Yard were engaged in investigations on the spot within an hour after the discovery, no clue as to the whereabouts of the murderer has yet been found.' On arrival they did not enter the room. They waited in expectation of the attendance of a pair of bloodhounds to track the murderer's scent. Unknown to the waiting police officers, one of the dogs, Burgho, had been returned to its owner, Edwin Brough of Scarborough. He had become impatient with the protracted financial wrangling over fees and insurance with Scotland Yard and was horrified to learn that in September Superintendent Arnold had attempted to use the other hound, Barnaby, to track a burglar. Brough's fear was that a burglar would have no compunction in killing or injuring a hound to avoid capture. The day before Kelly's murder Sir Charles Warren had instructed veterinary surgeon Alfred Sewell, who was acting on Brough's behalf, that Scotland Yard had finally obtained Home Office permission to finance use of the bloodhounds and an agreement could be drawn up. The agreement was duly drawn up but never signed. Both bloodhounds were back with their owner by 9 November.

After the futile delay, and acting on Superintendent Arnold's instructions, the door was forced open by McCarthy at 1.30 p.m. Doctors and police entered the room to examine its horrific contents and the inquiries into Kelly's murder began. Abberline found a man's clay pipe in the room, but on inquiry Barnett informed him that he smoked it. On the night of Saturday 10 November, a *Sunday Times* representative interviewed McCarthy and Bowyer in McCarthy's chandler's shop at 27 Dorset Street. McCarthy said:

> I instructed my man John [sic] Bowyer, here, to go to Mary Jane Kelly's room, and try and obtain some rent. She was charged 4s. per week, but was 30s. in arrears. It is a rule to collect the rent from the Court daily, but, as Kelly had been having a hard time of late, I had heard, I didn't press her. 'Go to No. 13,' I said to Bowyer, meaning Kelly's room, and see if she's going

to give me any money. Bowyer went, but when he knocked at the door he couldn't get an answer. Thinking it strange he looked through the keyhole and found the key missing. There are two windows that face the court on the left hand side of the room. One of them was broken when Kelly had her row with the man she said was her husband, and the hole had been stopped with a man's old coat, behind a muslin curtain. Bowyer put his hand through the hole, and drew aside the curtain and the coat. Although the man had been a soldier 20 years, and has seen service in India, he will tell you himself that he nearly fainted at the horrible sight that met his eyes. The woman was lying, a naked, bloody mass upon the bed, and mutilated out of all recognition.

The reporter then queried Bowyer, 'a somewhat sharp featured man with a coal begrimed visage,' who corroborated McCarthy's statement and said:

I was that scared at what I saw that when I could keep my knees from knocking under me I ran round to the governor here, and told him something dreadful had happened at No. 13. How anybody could have had the audacity to commit such a crime in such a place fairly knocked me all of a heap. Why, that 'ere court's nothing but a trap. There's only one entrance to it from the street as you have seen, sir, and that's as narrer as the opening to a sentry box!

'Yes,' chimed in Mr McCarthy,

the daring of the thing has surprised everybody who knows this neighbourhood. Day and night Dorset Street is never deserted. When the pub'ho's close lodging houses begin to get busy. That big one over the way, kept by Crossingham, and called the 'Commercial Street Chambers,' is open all night, and it exactly faces the entrance to my court. Yet nobody saw any strange man go down or come out of it. At the time we suppose the murder to have been committed the street must have been getting quite lively with people going to the Spitalfields Market. The police, too, I know are regular enough in their visits to the place; but they never heard the slightest sound to raise their suspicions. When Bowyer came running into me [sic] all scared and trembling, I went to No. 13 and put my head through the broken window. I haven't broken my fast since then; the sight made me sick, and it will be many a year before I forget it.[3]

A hurried, one-day inquest was held on Monday 12 November by coroner Dr Roderick Macdonald, at the Shoreditch town hall. Officers in attendance included Reid, Abberline, Nairn, and Chandler. The witnesses gave their evidence, including Kelly's lover, Joseph Barnett, and the inevitable verdict of murder by person or persons unknown was reached.

Barnett stated that Kelly had lived with a man named 'Morganstone' opposite Stepney Gas Works,[4] and after that with a Joseph Flemming. 'Morganstone' has never been positively identified, but a few clues as to his possible identity have now come to light. One of the newspaper reports on the inquest quoted Barnett as saying that 'Morganstone' worked at Stepney Gas Works.[5] No staff records of the Stepney Gas Company appear to have survived. The census returns were then checked, and in the 1881 census for 43 Fulham Road the family of Morgestern was shown, with the head, Adrienus L. Morgestern, thirty-three years old, a gas stoker, and his brother Maria A. Morgestern, twenty-six years old, also a gas stoker of the same address. Both were born in Alphen, Priel, The Netherlands. Given Morgestern's occupation of gas stoker, it would seem possible that we have found the 'Morganstone' so long sought. The census return for 1891 disclosed that the family no longer lived at the address.

That evening a new witness emerged. George Hutchinson called at Commercial Street Police Station to say that he had seen Kelly in the early hours of the day of her murder. More than that, she was in the company of a strange man, and Hutchinson was 'surprised to see a man so well dressed in her company.' He carefully observed the man, whom he described as 'about 34 or 35, height 5ft. 6in, complexion pale, dark eyes and eye lashes, slight moustache curled up each end and hair dark, very surly looking; Jewish appearance,' and stated that he could identify him. Abberline interrogated Hutchinson and was convinced that he was telling the truth. Hutchinson stated that the man he saw was carrying a pair of brown kid gloves in his right hand and that he 'walked very softly.' He said:

> I believe that he lives in the neighbourhood, and I fancied that I saw him in Petticoat Lane on Sunday morning, but I was not certain. I have been to the Shoreditch mortuary and recognised the body as that of the woman Kelly, whom I saw at two o'clock on Friday morning. Kelly did not seem to me to be drunk, but was a little bit spreeish. I was quite sober, not having had anything to drink all day. After I left the court I walked about all night, as

the place where I usually sleep was closed. I came in as soon as it opened in the morning. I am able to fix the time, as it was between ten and five minutes to two o'clock as I came by Whitechapel Church. When I left the corner of Miller's-court the clock struck three. One policeman went by the Commercial-street end of Dorset-street while I was standing there, but not one came down Dorset-street. I saw one man go into a lodging-house in Dorset-street, and no one else. I have been looking for the man all day.[6]

Soon after the Kelly murder Reid arrested a man who resembled a description that had been circulated of someone who had been seen in the vicinity of the recent murders. He was carrying a shiny black bag that was secured with a padlock. The man was arrested in Brick Lane and taken to Commercial Street Police Station and his bag searched. It contained a variety of artefacts stolen from Old St Pancras church and rather than being Jack the Ripper the man was a jeweller named George Bartlett. Nevertheless, Reid was commended by the magistrate for the, 'intelligence and activity' he had shown in capturing Bartlett.[7]

The house-to-house search following the Miller's Court murder took in a common lodging house in Paternoster Row. Deputy keeper Mary Cusins reported that a cigar maker named Joseph Isaacs had stayed at her lodging house for three to four days prior to the murder but disappeared immediately afterwards. Cusins remembered that on the night of the murder she heard him 'walk about his room,'[8] and lodger Cornelius Oakes stated that Isaacs often changed his dress and was heard to threaten violence to all women over the age of seventeen.[9] Furthermore, Isaacs allegedly resembled the description of the suspect given by Hutchinson.[10]

On 17 November, Swedish traveller Nikaner Benelius entered the house of a married woman, Harriet Rowe. When asked what he wanted, Benelius just grinned. He had been questioned previously in connection with the Berner Street murder. His story that he just wanted to ask Rowe, whose door had been left open, directions to Fenchurch Street tallied with the fact that he asked PC Imhoff directions to Fenchurch Street post office after leaving Rowe's house.

Speaking to the press about the incident, Reid said:

the man's innocence of any hand in the murders has been fully established. The man who has been a lodger at a German lodging-house at 90 Great Eastern Street, has been preaching in the streets, and behaving in a manner which suggests that he is not so fully responsible for his actions as he might be. It was therefore thought advisable to make the fullest inquiries, which have quite cleared him. He was arrested on suspicion in connection with the Berners-street [sic] murder, and is likely to be arrested every time the public attention is strained to the point of suspecting every man of odd behaviour.[11]

Joseph Isaacs returned to the lodgings on 6 December to collect a violin bow and then made his way to Drury Lane, where he stole a gold watch worth 30 shillings from a customer in a shop. He was arrested and taken to Bow Street Police Station before being collected by Inspector Abberline 'in a cab which was strongly escorted.'[12] He was detained at H Division headquarters, Leman Street, and the press reported that 'officials deny any knowledge of the arrest although the man is understood to be detained there.'[13]

One enterprising newspaper reported that Abberline 'was heard to say to one of his subordinates, 'keep this one quiet; we have got the right man at last. This is a big thing." '[14] The optimism, however, was short-lived. It emerged that Isaacs was not connected with the murders. He was suspected of an attack on prostitute Annie Farmer at a common lodging house on 20 November, but as for the Miller's Court murder, 'as far as can be ascertained the man could be in no way connected with that outrage.'[15]

Suggestions poured in from the public as to the identity of the murderer. A Dr 'Roslyn' Stephenson accused a Dr Morgan Davies of the London Hospital, having seen him re-enact the murderer's methods whilst Stephenson was a patient there. He said that Davies 'is himself a woman-hater. Although a man of powerful frame, and, according to the lines on his sallow face, of strong sexual passions.'

Stephenson made an arrangement with a man named George Marsh, according to which Marsh would pay Stephenson half of any reward received after the conviction of Dr Davies for wilful murder. Marsh had met regularly with Stephenson after the latter's discharge from hospital. Stephenson was then living in a common lodging house in Whitechapel. and according to Marsh was 'what I call a regular soaker—can drink from 8 o'clock in the morning until closing time but keep a clear head.' Marsh appeared to think that Stephenson was a better suspect than the man he proposed.

Stephenson undoubtedly figured briefly as a contemporary suspect as a result of Marsh's allegation and Stephenson also wrote a letter to the City Police on 16 October 1888 regarding his theory of the Ripper being a Frenchman. This extended to an article in the *Pall Mall Gazette* on 1 December 1888 along the same lines but anonymously credited as 'By One Who Thinks He Knows.' Stephenson went into Scotland Yard on 26 December 1888 and was seen by Inspector Thomas Roots who had, apparently, known him for some twenty years. Roots dismissed both Dr Davies and Stephenson himself as credible Ripper suspects. Stephenson went by the name 'Roslyn D'Onston' for many years after the murders eventually dying, aged seventy-six, at Islington Infirmary on 9 October 1916.

One suspect who appeared to have been taken quite seriously was Pierce John Robinson, who was reported to the police by his business partner, Richard Wingate. Robinson reacted suspiciously while talking about the murders and was keen to sell his share of the business and go to America. Scotland Yard's Superintendent Waghorn went to Suffolk to investigate on 22 January 1889, and reported that Robinson was a religious maniac who claimed to have some medical training. Superintendent Arnold and Sergeant Thick took up the inquiry and found that Robinson had lived in the Mile End Road. He had married bigamously, for which he was sentenced to four months at the Central Criminal Court. He had left the Mile End Road on 1 November 1888, however, and was proved to be in Suffolk on the night of the Kelly murder.

The unease and strife at the senior level of the Metropolitan Police Force was further evinced with the resignation of Sir Charles Warren, which was announced on the very day of the Kelly murder. This was the result of his ongoing bad relations with the Home Office—Matthews in particular—and was precipitated by the publication of an article in *Murray's Magazine* on the policing of the metropolis. This article was published without Home Office sanction and simply brought matters to a head. James Monro succeeded him in office.

With the murders now attracting such widespread attention and importance, the Queen herself was updated on the progress of government action in relation to them. In a letter to Queen Victoria dated 10 November 1888, the Prime Minister, the Marquis of Salisbury, wrote: 'At Cabinet today it was resolved to issue a proclamation offering free pardon to anyone who should give Evidence as to the recent murder Except the actual perpetrator of the crime.'[16]

CHAPTER ELEVEN

The Great Silk Robberies

'He was a London detective, whom everybody learned to admire, even the criminals he brought to justice.'

The Weekly Dispatch

Despite having his hands full with the Whitechapel murders in the autumn of 1888, Reid was able to leave the direction of the inquiry to Scotland Yard, represented by the more-than-able Abberline. Throughout the period of the murders Reid gave his attention to a variety of major crimes that were still being committed in the East End including attempted murder, poisoning, bigamy, fraud, illegal gambling and the selling of obscene photographs. In one case he excelled himself. It gives an illuminating insight into the East End underworld.

On Friday 23 November 1888, Maurice Bushell, a clerk at Messrs. Pattinson & Sons, Silk and General Agents of 21 Bread Street, Cheapside, was expecting the delivery of a large consignment of silk and velvet from Germany worth £1,800. Walter Evans, a licensed carman of Butcher's Row, Ratcliff, had sent one of his carmen, William Lee, to Blackfriars Station on the Friday afternoon to catch the London-Dover train and collect the silk. It was to be delivered to various addresses in the City, including Pattinson & Sons.

At 7.40 p.m. Lee returned with the news that he had lost his van. He told Evans that he had stopped at Mill's Coffee House in Leman Street, Whitechapel, at about 7.15 p.m., after delivering four of the thirteen packages he had collected. Lee put the nosebag on the horse and secured the van by putting a chain on the wheel and taking the drag chain off.

While he drank tea with another carman named Leverett he was told that his van had been stolen.

Lee immediately reported the theft at Leman Street Police Station, before searching the area for his van. The van was recovered later that night about a mile away, but only two of the nine cases were still on it. Leverett's van had not been stolen, and Lee presumed that this was because Leverett had a van boy mind his load whilst he did not. Although he had been facing the window in the coffee shop in order to watch his van, he later explained, 'you could see the van and yet you could not; it was dark; you could see the shadow of the van.'

On Sunday, 25 November, at 11.30 a.m., carman Joseph Avis, a former employee of Walter Evans, who had been sacked two years previously for stealing horse feed, was in Whitechapel Road, talking to his father when he was beckoned by coffee shop owner Henry Fife. Fife asked Avis if he had heard anything about the 'squeeze' (silk) that had recently been stolen. Avis, having read about the theft in the newspaper, had just been talking about it with his father.

'It was an all right job, wasn't it?' Fife said. 'The carmen got on all right didn't they? They got £100 a piece before they went into the coffee shop. Will you come along with me and see it?' Avis declined the offer as he was with his father but agreed to meet him that evening in his coffee shop in Baker's Row, Whitechapel. The story got back to Walter Evans, but when challenged Lee denied receiving £100. Walter Evans believed him and continued to employ Lee and Leverett, saying, 'If there was a breath of suspicion on them I would not employ them. We still employ them—we have no reason to distrust them.'

Avis told his story to another of Evans' carmen, John Leyton, and the pair went to Fife's coffee house at about 6 p.m. Avis told Fife that Leyton worked for Carter Pattersons and that he had two rolls of dark melton cloth, each measuring about 150 yards, that he wanted to sell to Fife. 'Did you hear about the squeeze that was lost?' Fife asked Leyton. 'It was got away clear. The carman had money to go into the coffee shop, while the other people took the load away. There were two carmen in it, and they were paid £100 to go into the coffee shop.' He added that he could get rid of a load at any time for Leyton, and that the same man who drove Lee's load away would do the same for him. Fife obviously had great faith in the dishonesty of carmen.

It was not mere honesty that had prompted Avis's actions; he was a man bearing a grudge. Some years earlier Avis himself had stolen a load of flour from a van:

I drove the van to Fife's house—he did not buy it, but he asked the man next door to buy it at 8 p.m. and I was arrested at nine next morning—the policemen were not in Fife's house when he refused to buy, but a detective was. If Fife had not given information I should not have been arrested, and I bear enmity against him.

For this Avis had received an eighteen months' sentence at the Surrey Sessions. He had previously served four months for stealing 174 lb of wool from the Albert Dock. After his release Avis still frequented Fife's coffee shop. He still 'spoke to Fife in a friendly way, and said, "Fife, you ought not to have put me away," although I had a grudge against him.' Avis hoped to kill two birds with one stone: to see Fife sent down and to get into Walter Evans' good books as he would soon need a job, having been given a week's notice for slackness by his current employer. The following morning Avis and Leyton told their story to Walter Evans, Sergeant Stephen White, and Inspector Reid, who had been given charge of the case on the previous day. The resourceful Reid hatched a plan that was implemented the same day.

Avis and Leyton met Fife at The Grasshopper Public House, taking a sample of the cloth Leyton had to sell. They told the unsuspecting Fife that they had sold one of the rolls for £7 but still had the other if he was interested. Fife said he would go to Leyton's house to measure the cloth, and if it was all there he would give them £7 for it. He would bring someone with him to carry it away. When Leyton told him that he lived at 107 Harford Street, Fife expressed concern, as he thought that a lot of policemen lived in the area. Leyton assured him that this was not the case. Before parting Fife flashed a gold watch before Avis's eyes, boasting that he had sold one for £25 and would sell Avis another for just £5.

The following day, Tuesday, Avis met Fife in The Grave Maurice Public House opposite the London Hospital and asked him if he wanted to take a load, explaining that Leyton was going to take a load out of Wood Street, Cheapside, to the London and North Western Railway. When asked where Leyton was loading up, Avis told him 'at Bennett's in Cheapside, and Silber and Flemings in Wood Street.' They met up again at 2 p.m. that afternoon in New Road to arrange getting someone to drive Leyton's load of jewellery and mantles away. On Wednesday morning Avis met Fife again and asked him if he could take the load that day. Fife said he could and sent Avis to The Market House Pub in Nile Street, where he was to ask for a carman named George Saunders, the very man who had driven off William Lee's load.

Avis duly told Saunders that his mate had got 'a good load of stuff' he wanted to be rid of. A deal was struck.

'Is it the carman?' Saunders asked.

'Yes,' Avis replied.

'What does the load contain?'

'Mantles and jewellery.'

'Is it a straightforward job?' queried Saunders.

'Yes,' was the reply.

'Mind you, if this is wrong, off comes your head,' warned Saunders.

The threat was reinforced when Saunders showed Avis a revolver. Later that afternoon, at the Madhouse pub in City Road, Saunders and Avis met with Thomas Cook, Saunders warning, 'Keep your eyes open while we go on the business.' Avis and Saunders went to the street where Leyton was supposed to be waiting for them but he was not there. They waited for twenty minutes before Leyton finally arrived. Avis climbed into the back of the van and Saunders mounted the front and drove away.

Reid, White, and Detective Constable Dalbin had borrowed the van and filled it with a bogus load. They followed the van along the streets until it stopped and Saunders and Avis disembarked. Reid walked past them and heard Saunders say to another man, 'Won't be long.' Saunders then drove the van to Church Street, Hoxton, and pulled up at some stables. He opened a door and a goat ran out. Reid was observing from the gardens of a nearby Board School until Avis and Saunders began to unload the van. Reid called to DC Dalbin and they entered the stable yard. They saw Saunders with his hat and coat off; Avis promptly ran off, having played his part in Reid's plan. Reid took hold of Saunders and handed him to Sergeant White. 'I know nothing of this,' Saunders protested; 'a man asked me to lend him a hand to unload the van; I know nothing of this nor yet of the cloth.'

Upon searching the stables Reid found several packages that had been taken from the van, two ledgers printed in Russian, and a bottle of preserves, which was part of the proceedings of a van robbery in the City on 20 November.

Thomas Cook entered the yard, asking, 'Who let my goat out?' Reid, recognising him, as he had known him for years, asked, 'Is this your stable?'

'Yes, and everything in it,' Cook replied.

'Then you will be arrested for having stolen property,' said Reid.

'That is a nice thing is it not? I let part of my stable to a scamp and I know nothing of this property,' protested Cook.

'Never mind about this property,' Reid replied; 'this is not stolen, it is only lent.'

Reid found that Cook owned a shop around the corner from the stables in Cropley Street. He went there with Sergeant White and DC Dalbin, and on entering saw behind the counter several bundles that turned out to be a sealskin dolman and other stolen property, including 240 skins of leather. Reid saw boot manufacturer Alfred Dodd in the workshop and asked him who he was. 'I am Mr. Cook's partner,' Dodd replied, so Sergeant White promptly arrested him for possession of stolen goods.

Dodd handed Reid a purse, saying, 'Cook handed this to me through the clicker when the policemen were taking him by the door.' Upon opening the purse Reid found that it contained £36 in gold and a £10 note. Dodd was taken to the police station while Reid searched Cook's house, which was opposite the shop. Reid was accompanied and assisted by Cook's partner, Mrs Hitchin, who went by the name of Mrs Cook. 'You will find nothing down here,' she told Reid; 'I am very glad it has come to this, for I am tired of it; you had better go upstairs, you will find something there.'

Reid forced the door of a back room at the top of the house and found a veritable treasure trove of stolen property that included twenty-four boxes of velvet and plush, seven boxes of lace and embroidery, mantles, a curtain, silk, and 380 parcel carriers. In the kitchen was a large amount of leather and in the shop were mirrors, shoes, boots, dresses, harnesses, lamps, weights, lace, and two whips. A search of the bedroom revealed two ladies' jackets, three dolmans, a rug, and various other items of clothing. In a silk shirt £2. 12s. 6d. was found in a pocket. The property was packed by the police, and Reid loaded the stolen property into a van and drove it to Kingsland Police Station, where Cook, Dodd, and Saunders were in custody. He spoke with Cook.

'I have searched your house and found what I have been looking for, a quantity of silk and velvet stolen from Mr. Evans last Friday night,' Reid told him.

'My God! That is a nice thing. I let those two top rooms to a man some weeks ago, and I had no idea what he had got there,' persisted Cook.

'That you will have to prove,' said Reid laconically.

Reid went to arrest Fife at his coffee house in Baker's Row at 1 a.m. on the Friday morning. Henry Fife's reputation as a handler of stolen goods was well known to him. Reid knocked on the door calling out, 'All right, Harry, open the door, quick.' Fife opened the door. He was not wearing a night-shirt but gave the impression of having been in bed. 'You have made a great mistake this time,' Fife said; 'whoever gave you this information is wrong.'

More of the gang's hoard was found: three new carpet mats, one seal-skin bag, one new conductor's leather bag, and a piece of plush. On the way to the police station Fife further stated, 'If I had known you had been there I should not have been here.' DC Dalbin understood him to mean that he would have bolted had he known the police had come for him.

Maurice Bushell of Messrs. Pattinson & Sons identified his missing goods at the police station, as did George Carter, whose barrow containing seventy-two pairs of unmade boots had been stolen on 8 November when he paid a visit to a beer shop. Charles Badham, whose van had been stolen on 20 November when he delivered a case of books, was reunited with his two stolen cases. It was estimated that between October and November 1888 Henry Fife, George Saunders, Thomas Cook, and Alfred Dodd had conspired to steal over £5,000 worth of goods, a very considerable sum in 1888.

Henry Fife had a novel alibi for his whereabouts on the night of 23 November, when William Lee's load had been stolen. He claimed to have been at Commercial Street Police Station accusing a man of being Jack the Ripper. Reid did not know if this was true, but after Fife was charged Reid said, '[he] has never since suggested at the time the theft took place he was at the police station charging a person with murder.'

The case went to the Old Bailey. Frank Skeete, a shoemaker from Hackney, was also involved in the incident. He remembered that on 23 November,

I was at Fife's coffee-house, and about 6 o'clock a man came in and asked Fife to cook him a piece of meat—he said 'certainly' and asked him if he had got the meat with him; and he acted in such a suspicious manner that I followed him out, and Fife followed me, and I went up to him in Dorset Street and gave him in charge, and we all went to Commercial Street police station; it was then about 7.30—the charge was preferred against him, and he was detained till inquiries were made—I don't know whether he was liberated at 8.30—I will swear that from 6.30 to 8.30 Fife was in my company.

By chance H Division Detective Thomas Stacey was in the same court in connection with another case when the question of Fife's alibi arose. Stacey confirmed that the incident had taken place:

I was at the station a month ago, when Fife came in with two men, one of whom Fife pointed out as having acted very suspiciously, and he was charged with behaving in such a manner that [DC Walter] Dew thought he might be the Whitechapel murderer—he was brought in between seven and eight—he was detained and afterwards discharged on the ground that he was suffering from religious mania—Fife was, I believe, not present when he was discharged—Fife said that he had followed him for some time, or 'a long time'—it may have been after eight o'clock when Fife left.

Inspector Walter Beck of H Division added:

I was on duty in the charge room on November 23rd—it is my duty to enter in the occurrence book the particulars of the visits of persons who come to the station—this entry is in my writing—
    'On November 23rd at 6.45 a man was brought to the station by the police who was supposed from his conduct in the street to be the Whitechapel murderer.'
    There is not a doubt that Fife came to the station to give information.

George Saunders received a prison sentence of seven years, Henry Fife got five years, and Thomas Cook ten years. Their protestations of innocence had failed. No evidence was offered against Alfred Dodd and he was therefore discharged. Reid was complimented by the common sergeant who said that there was no doubt that the trap which was prepared for the prisoners was one of the most skilfully laid plans they had heard of for a long time. Reid, White and Dalbin all received rewards and the grand jury addressed 'a letter of commendation of his cleverness' to Reid. Some of the recovered silk belonged to a Spanish firm, and the Spanish Royal Naval Commissioner sent Reid a letter of thanks.[1]

Reid had been simultaneously working on the Whitechapel murders and great silk robberies. While the case of the silk robbers had been successfully concluded the threat of further Whitechapel murders was ever present. Six weeks after murder of Mary Jane Kelly, Reid investigated another suspicious person. Twenty-four-year-old Theophil Hanhart, a French and German teacher from a school near Bath, confessed to a constable 'that he was the cause of the Whitechapel murders, and he was very uneasy in his mind about it.' The Reverend W. Mathias said that Hanhart had been in his care since 16 September, 'and from that date he had never been out of his sight.' Reid stated that he was 'satisfied that the prisoner could not have committed the murders,' and he was subsequently sent to the Shoreditch infirmary.[2]

The close of 1888 saw another murder added to the East End tally, that of Rose Mylett, whose body was found by PC Robert Goulding at 4.15 a.m. on 20 December 1888, in Clarke's Yard, Poplar. There was no throat cutting or mutilation, and the doctors decided that she had been strangled. There was, however, disagreement on this, Dr Thomas Bond feeling that it was accidental choking caused by her collar. Both the medical evidence and the timing of witness sightings, of Mylett with suspect men shortly before her death, leave little doubt that she was indeed murdered. The inquest was held and a verdict of murder by person or persons unknown was returned. Assistant Commissioner Dr Robert Anderson felt that it was not murder and later claimed that it was only because of the Ripper scare that it was suggested as such.

CHAPTER TWELVE

'Clay Pipe' Alice

'People in those days had what might be described as the Jack the Ripper complex. Immediately a murder and mutilation was reported, they jumped to the conclusion that he was the culprit.'

Detective Constable Walter Dew

Thoughts that the East End was free of the Ripper's grim shadow were dashed on Wednesday 17 July 1889. At 12.50 a.m. that day PC Walter Andrews, on patrol, discovered the body of Alice McKenzie, a prostitute, lying on the pavement in Castle Alley, Whitechapel, with her throat cut. The only person in the vicinity was Isaac Lewis Jacob, seen by PC Andrews when he blew his whistle. Jacob, of 12 New Castle Place, was walking towards Wentworth Street with a plate in his hand, going, he said, to get something for his supper. Superintendent Arnold, Chief Inspector West and Reid were soon upon the scene of the murder and Reid recorded all the details. In little more than an hour Chief Commissioner James Monro and Colonel Bolton Monsell attended the scene.

Reid gave evidence at the inquest, held at the Working Lads' Institute, Whitechapel, before coroner Wynne Baxter, on Thursday 18 July. He described how he learned of the murder:

I received the call at five minutes past one o'clock on Wednesday morning. I dressed and ran down at once. On arriving at Castle Alley, I found the Wentworth Street end blocked by a policeman. At the back of the baths I saw the deceased. The doctor had not arrived. I saw a cut on the left side of the throat of the dead woman; a quantity of blood under the head, which ran into the gutter towards Wentworth Street. Her clothes were raised, and her face was slightly turned towards the road. She was lying on her back. I felt her face and body, and found they were warm. Dr Phillips came, and the superintendent, Mr Arnold, soon after. At the time I ascertained that the Whitechapel end of the alley was blocked. The deputy, superintendent, and his wife at the Whitechapel Baths, and also the engineer, were interviewed, and they stated they knew nothing. After the doctor had examined the body it was placed on the police ambulance. Underneath the body was found the pipe produced. It is a broken clay pipe.

Baxter: Was there blood on it?

Reid: Yes. There was also some unburned tobacco. I also found a bronze farthing.

Baxter: Was there also blood on the farthing?

Reid: Yes. Inquiries were continued. I produce a correct plan of Castle Alley which I have examined. During the whole time from the finding of the body until its removal there was no civilian present, except the witness Jacobs, everything having been done very quietly.

Reid explained that

the fence shown on the plan opposite the place where the body laid was about ten feet high, apparently having been erected to block the windows of the cottages. On the path on the east side of the alley there was a row of costermonger's barrows. The two vans close to where the woman was were chained together. There were altogether five lamps, one of them near the wagons.

Baxter: Would any stranger be likely to find Castle Alley unless they knew the locality?

Reid: It is approached by a narrow covered passage from High Street. I don't think a stranger would go down the alley unless he was taken.

Baxter: There would be people still about in the High Street?

Reid: Oh yes, all night. Two police constables are continually passing through this alley all night. It is hardly ever left alone for five minutes. Although it is called an alley, it is a narrow court leading into a broad turning, with two narrow exits. Any person looking upon it from the Wentworth Street end would regard it as a blind street. No stranger would think he could pass through it, and none but foot passengers can.

Baxter: You saw the body removed?

Reid: Yes.

Baxter: Was the pavement wet?

Reid: Yes, it was raining when it was removed.

Baxter: Was it raining when you arrived?

Reid: Yes a very little.

Baxter: Was the spot on which the deceased was lying dry?

Reid: Yes, except where there was blood. The rain came on about a quarter to one a.m.

Baxter: Is there any doubt about the name of the deceased as far as you know?

Reid: No. I have since made inquiries in Gun Street and ascertained from the deputy, Ryder, that Mogg Cheeks, the woman mentioned yesterday, stayed with her sister all night, explaining her absence from the lodging house. I searched the deceased at the mortuary. Her clothing was in filthy condition, and I think she was one of the lowest type. I have no doubt that the deed was committed on the exact spot where the woman was found. I should think she was lying on the pavement, with the head towards High Street, and near the kerb, about two feet away from the wall. No person, unless they went along the pathway, could have seen the body.

Baxter: Was that in consequence of the position of the lamp?

Reid: Yes, and the shadow of the vans screened it. Any person going along the road would not have seen it. It was necessary to use the constable's lamp to ascertain whether the woman's throat was cut.

Jury: Do you consider that the place was sufficiently lighted?

Reid: Yes; there were five lamps, but there were shadows of the vans.

Foreman: In previous cases was any similar coin found as that which you picked up in this instance?

Reid: In the Hanbury Street case two farthings were found.

Foreman: Is it possible that the coin was passed off in the dark for a half sovereign?

Reid: I should think for a sixpence. The tobacco in the pipe had not been lighted. It was an old pipe termed in the lodging houses 'a nose warmer.'

Baxter: Was there only one case in which a farthing was found?

Reid: The Hanbury Street case is the only one I remember.

The pipe was

. . . a short clay pipe, and this at first pointed to the conclusion that the murderer was a member of the lower classes, and not in a superior position to them. The pipe, however, appears to have belonged to the woman herself, evidence having been given that she was a regular smoker of pipes, which were borrowed, although she purchased her own tobacco.

Her nickname was 'Clay Pipe Alice.'[1]

Reid accompanied the body to the mortuary and there searched it. There was a zigzag-shaped cut on her abdomen. Dr Bagster Phillips was summoned but after examining the body decided that 'the wounds had not been inflicted by the same hand as in the previous cases, inasmuch as the injuries in this case are not so severe and the cut on the stomach is not so direct.' Again Dr Bond was called in to give his opinion and disagreed with Phillips' conclusion, reporting that he found 'in this murder evidence of similar design to the former Whitechapel murders.' This would appear to have influenced the Chief Commissioner, James Monro, when he reported to the Home Office the same day:

I need not say that every effort will be made by the Police to discover the murderer, who, I am inclined to believe is identical with the notorious 'Jack the Ripper' of last year. It will be seen that in spite of ample police precautions and vigilance the assassin has again succeeded in committing a murder and getting off without leaving the slightest clue to his identity.

Dr Bagster Phillips noted in his post mortem report:

While searching the clothing one of the attendants found a short pipe, well used, which he thoughtlessly threw onto the ground & broke it. I had the pieces put on one side meaning to preserve them but up to the time of writing this report they have not been recovered by me.

Phillips' conclusions after his examination were clear:

After careful and long deliberation I cannot satisfy myself on purely anatomical & professional grounds that the Perpetrator of all the 'WhChl. murders' is one man. I am on the contrary impelled to a contrary conclusion. This noting the mode of procedure & the character of the mutilations & judging of motive in connection with the latter.

I do not here enter into the comparison of the cases neither do I take into account what I admit may be almost conclusive evidence in favour of the one man theory if all the surrounding circumstances & other evidence are considered.

Dr Thomas Bond demurred and felt that this was another Ripper murder. At the final inquest hearing the usual verdict of murder by person or persons unknown was returned.

A diversion was caused for the police when a drunken criminal, William Wallace Brodie, gave himself up at Leman Street Police Station for this and the previous murders. Reid took his statement, but after much inquiry he was cleared of suspicion.

It may be appropriate to note here that Inspector Abberline ended his official position as head of the inquiries into the murders in early 1889 and was succeeded by his colleague, Inspector Henry Moore, who had accompanied Abberline from the start of the investigation. Abberline's departure from the investigation was marked by a rather large claim he submitted on 5 February 1889, 'for expenses in connection with the Whitechapel murders, £39. 6. 1.'[2]

The newspapers, like the inquest jury, made much of the farthing found under the body. The *Daily Telegraph* noted that

> underneath the body was found a bloodstained farthing. To this discovery only a vague reference was made in yesterday's issue, as it was considered undesirable to give publicity at that time to the circumstance. The assumption is that this farthing was given to the deceased by her murderer in the same way as similar coins were passed upon the Hanbury-street victim as half-sovereigns, it was believed, for in that instance they had been brightly polished. The farthing discovered under the body of M'Kenzie was, on the contrary, dull and dirty, and it was difficult to explain why the man should have tried to foist it upon the woman as a coin of higher value under the light of the gaslamp, which would have enabled her at once to detect the fraud. One explanation of this matter is that the man may have given the woman the coin on the road to Castle-alley, probably in the dark passage which leads from High-street, Whitechapel. It is open to doubt whether he meant her to understand that it was a half-sovereign or a sixpence. Inspector Reid inclines to the opinion that it was passed as a sixpence. The farthing is considered by some as affording a certain clue to the identity of the murderer, as it may provide an indication as to his position in life.[3]

Soon after the McKenzie murder an interview appeared in the London *Evening News* which did not name its source but the 'Chief of the Criminal Investigation Department' may well have been Reid himself:

THE WHITECHAPEL MURDER
Interview With a Chief of the Criminal Investigation Department

A short time ago I had an opportunity—I need not tell where—of making the acquaintance of one of the officers who had under his control the body of detectives . . . to seek in Whitechapel the notorious woman slayer. My friend the detective was more inclined to reflect than to 'air' his theories.

'To begin,' said he in response to my continued asking, 'we know as little of the murder as the public, that is to say, absolutely nothing.'

'I find that somewhat dispiriting.'

'Yes, and heaven only knows the anxiety and endless worry of the time to the detective force. No stone was left unturned. We followed out the suggestions of the public. We searched every house in Whitechapel and interrogated closely every occupant.'

'And to no purpose?' I interrupted.

'None, we could find no trace.'

'And what is your own idea as to the murderer's identity?'

'My firm impression,' observed the detective chief, 'is that a low sneak, with terribly developed homicidal tendencies, is the man 'wanted.' He lives in Whitechapel, of that I am confident. His knowledge of the locality is astonishing. But of course all is really conjecture.'

'You do not suspect the 'absent sailor' theory?'

'By no means. If by chance one of my men catches the murderer red-handed, believe me I feel confident it will be found that on a previous occasion I have interrogated him in one of the Whitechapel houses. And this must convey to you some idea as to what we have had to work upon as clues, and how purposeless it is to arrest suspicious characters when we possess not a tittle of evidence against any of them.'

'But you had one important clue, the handwriting at the staircase foot in Goulstone-street [sic]?' I could see I was now touching an awkward point, and that the detective chief looked as if he would 'hedge' somewhat. He admitted having seen the handwriting, and although he hardly justified Sir Charles Warren's order for its instant deletion, yet he firmly believed that a rising against the Jews in Whitechapel would have resulted on the following Sunday when the news got bruited abroad.

To continue our further conversation upon other details would only be to elucidate points which have already been fully discussed elsewhere. What opinions the detective chief continues to hold after this recent murder he is not likely to divulge at the present juncture. Doubtless he still scouts the absent sailor theory and inclines to support the conviction of one of the most experienced police superintendents in London as expressed to me the other day, that the murderer belongs to the slaughterman class, one of the lowest types of men in our midst. 'They revel in blood' was the remark made to me, 'and they are deft with the knife.' However, it is very unfair to ridicule the police in the present crisis, because, as the detective chief truly observed, 'There has been nothing like these murders in the history of crime.'[4]

One foreign visitor to London in August 1889 was American journalist R. Harding Davis who, intrigued by the infamous murders, had arranged a visit to Scotland Yard, an interview with Assistant Commissioner Anderson and a tour of the Whitechapel area with Inspector Henry Moore. Anderson said to Davis, 'I don't think you will be disappointed in the district. After a stranger has gone over it he takes a much more lenient view of our failure to find Jack the Jack the Ripper, as they call him, than he did before.' Davis duly toured the district under the guidance of Moore who ended by pointing into the dark arches of the London, Tilbury and Southend Railway. He said to Davis, 'Now, what a place for a murder that would be.' Shortly afterwards when Davis was on his return voyage to the USA another murder victim was found under those very railway arches prompting Davis to ponder if the Ripper had been lurking near them that night and 'had acted on the inspector's suggestion', or whether the inspector himself was Jack the Ripper.[5]

CHAPTER THIRTEEN

The Pinchin Street Torso

> 'Yes, the Ripper had all the luck.'
>
> Commissioner Henry Smith, City Police

Two months after the murder of Alice McKenzie, at 5.15 a.m. on Tuesday 10 September 1889, PC William Pennett, whilst on patrol, discovered the headless and legless torso of a woman underneath the easternmost railway arch in Pinchin Street, St. George's-in-the-East, near the junction with Backchurch Lane. PC Pennett was a reliable officer and was to distinguish himself the following year, on 25 November, when he jumped into the River Thames at Tower Hill, in uniform, in order to rescue a man who was attempting to commit suicide. Pennett became 'a hero of the police' and was awarded the Silver Medal for this deed; he was soon promoted to sergeant.[1] It quickly became apparent that this was no Ripper murder, but that it was a method of disposing of a body. True, there was a gash across the abdomen, but this appeared to have been inflicted whilst dismembering the body and not as a result of any deliberate mutilation.

The effect on Reid of the discovery of yet another corpse in his division can only be guessed at. So many unsolved murders taking place in a relatively brief period must have been tremendously dispiriting. Nevertheless, upon hearing of the torso at Pinchin Street Reid immediately took up the investigation. He reported:

On receiving information of the discovery of Human Remains in Pinchin Street St Georges 10th inst I at once directed PS White to search the adjoining Railway Arches and other likely places in the neighbourhood with a view to trace the missing parts of the body also to make inquiries with a view to gain information as to who deposited the portion of body in the arch.

I also directed P.S. Thick to make inquiries at sheds, houses, and places where barrows are kept, or lent out on hire also at butchers in the neighbourhood of Pinchin Street with a view to gain any information regarding the matter.

I directed P.S. Godley to search information with a view to trace missing persons and the identification of the remains.

I also had telegrams sent to A.S. asking that search be at once made with a view to find the missing portions of the body.

I have also had several officers making inquiries in the neighbourhood of Pinchin Street with a view to gain any information respecting the above matter.

I asked the Inspr. of the dustcarts for the Parish of St. Georges to ask his men and direct them to report to him if any bloodstained clothes were taken from any house, and let police know at once. This was done and information was received from . . . stating that some had been found in Batty Street which is being inquired into.

Inquiries were made by Inspector Henry Moore regarding the bloodstained clothing and it was found that they were the result of a pregnancy confinement.

The London edition of the *New York Herald* carried a story with the startling headline: 'DOES HE KNOW THE RIPPER? WHO IS THIS MAN THAT CALLED AT THE 'HERALD' OFFICE SUNDAY.' The paper said that it had received information of the murder at 1.15 a.m. on the morning of the previous Sunday. A man calling himself John Cleary had called at the editorial offices and stated that there was another 'Ripper' murder in Backchurch Lane. It was investigated but proved to be without foundation, and the matter had no significance until the Tuesday morning when the remains were found. The newspaper also carried a long and detailed account of the discovery, reporting that the Chief Commissioner himself and Chief Constable Bolton Monsell were quickly on the scene and at the mortuary.

There was no clue as to the identity of the deceased, and the *Herald* speculated that the body might be that of an 'unhappy woman' named Lydia Hart, described as living in Ellen Street, off Backchurch Lane. The missing Lydia Hart was quickly located by her two sons and some friends at the local infirmary. She had been on 'a bit of a spree' and found it necessary to seek medical attention.

A reporter continued to make inquiries, visiting lodging houses as far afield as Thrawl Street and Osborn Street. He found that a Mrs Cornwall was missing from lodgings at North East Passage, 'a small narrow and dark' court leading off another, 'equally narrow and objectionable.' The piece then speculated that the remains might have been those of this woman. In the event, however, the police were unable to identify them. The *Herald* piece also listed the previous murders, with the first being shown as 'An unknown woman, Christmas week, 1887,' and the murder of Emma Smith in April 1888 totally omitted.[2]

The police were unable to trace the man Cleary, the address given being apparently false and lengthy inquiries ensued. Chief Inspector Swanson himself was engaged in these inquiries, and eventually the man was found to be John Arnold, a newsvendor, of 2 Harveys Buildings, Strand. He stated that he had been told of a murder in Backchurch Lane whilst walking in Fleet Street. He did not know the man who told him, and it would appear to have been a 'lark'. He had given the *Herald* the name 'John Kemp', not Cleary. The address he had given was a former one. Needless to say it was a gift for the press, who made much of it and trumpeted the new Whitechapel outrage.

Dr Phillips examined the remains and pronounced:

> I have not noticed any sufficient similarity to convince me it was the same person who committed both mutilations, but the division of the neck and the attempt to disarticulate the bones of the spine are very similar to that which was effected in this case. The savagery shown by the mutilated remains in the Dorset-street case far exceeded that shown in this case. The mutilations in the Dorset-street case were most wanton, whereas in this case it strikes me they were made for the purpose of disposing of the body. I think in this case there has been greater knowledge shown in regard to the construction of the parts composing the spine, and on the whole there has been a greater knowledge shown of how to separate a joint.

The police had received 'no information to afford a clue as to how the body was conveyed to the spot at which it was found & there being no doubt it was carried there either by Barrow or by some person on his back.' A Home Office letter said 'that not withstanding every precaution the murderer has been enabled to slip through our patrols, and dispose of the body of his victim without being observed by police.... 'We <u>must</u> put a stop to these Whitechapel outrages.'[3] Superintendent Arnold's only answer was to request another hundred officers 'for a couple of months.' The *Morning Advertiser* reported, 'The police by the mouth of Inspector Moore, frankly confesses that they have no clue.'[4]

The same newspaper offered a possible identification of the Pinchin Street victim as Emily Barker of Northampton. The girl was said to have led a wild life, and the last that had been heard of her was that she had been found on a doorstep in London in a semi-nude state by a missionary. She escaped from his charge two days before the discovery of the remains in Pinchin Street. Her mother stated that she was convinced the victim was her daughter, and that she had made the chemise her daughter was wearing and which was found wrapped round the remains. She further stated that her suspicions were confirmed by a mark on her finger. Emily Barker was under twenty years of age, however, and the remains were estimated by the medical men to be of an older woman.[5] The next day they reported that Scotland Yard had investigated Mrs Barker's claims and the remains were definitely not Emily Barker, who was only 5 feet 4 inches as opposed to the estimated five feet nine-ten inches of the victim.[6]

An inquest was held on the torso which concluded at St. George's Vestry Hall, Cable Street, on Tuesday 24 September. The now-familiar verdict of wilful murder against some person or persons unknown was reached. The unidentified remains were placed in a sealed tin vessel filled with spirit to preserve them. It was buried at 10 a.m. on 5 October at the East London Cemetery, Grange Park, Plaistow, in grave number 16185. The tin box bore a metal plate with the following legend: 'This case contains the body of a woman (unknown) found in Pinchin Street St. Georges-in-the-East 10th Septr./89.'

The celebrated alienist, Dr Lyttleton Stewart Forbes Winslow, who had taken an interest in the murders from the beginning now made public his views on the identity of Jack the Ripper. He wrote, with some confidence, 'If anyone can speak authoritatively on the subject I feel I can.' Winslow had his own theory and his mind was set. He claimed that he had found a clue:

> which I worked up to such a state of accuracy that I was enabled to trace the criminal after each of his previous murders. I found the address of the various lodgings he had occupied on the night of each of the murders. I have an exact description of the man in my possession. I know his haunts, his ways of living and his habits. He was a religious homicidal maniac.[7]

Forbes Winslow's theory was elaborated in the *New York Herald*, in September 1889 and a cutting was included in one of the now missing official files. The relevant material was photocopied, before its loss, in the 1970s:

THE WHITECHAPEL MURDERS

A report having been current that a man has been found who is quite convinced that 'Jack the Ripper' occupied rooms in his house, and that he had communicated his suspicions in the first instance to Dr. Forbes Winslow, together with detailed particulars, a reporter had an interview with the doctor yesterday afternoon on the subject. 'Here are Jack the Ripper's boots,' said the doctor, at the same time taking a large pair of boots from under his table. 'The tops of these boots are composed of ordinary cloth material, while the soles are made of indiarubber. The tops have great bloodstains on them.' The reporter put the boots on, and found they were completely noiseless. Besides these noiseless coverings the doctor says he has the 'Ripper's' ordinary walking boots, which are very dirty, and the man's coat which is also bloodstained. Proceeding, Dr. Winslow said that on the morning of Aug. 30 a woman with whom he was in communication was spoken to by a man in Worship Street, Finsbury. He asked her to come down a certain court with him, offering her £1. This she refused, and he then doubled the amount, which she also declined. He next asked her where the court led to, and shortly afterwards left. She told some neighbours, and the party followed the man for some distance. Apparently, he did not know that he was being followed, but when he and the party had reached the open street he turned round, raised his hat, and with an air of bravado said: 'I know what you have been doing; good morning.' The woman then watched the man into a certain house, the situation of which the doctor would not describe. She previously noticed the man because of his strange manner, and on the morning on which the woman Mackenzie was murdered (July 17) she saw him washing his hands in the yard of the house referred to. He was in his shirt-sleeves at the time, and had a very peculiar look upon his face. This was about four o'clock in the morning. The doctor said he was now waiting for a certain telegram, which was the only obstacle to his effecting the man's arrest. The supposed assassin lived with a friend of Dr. Forbes Winslow's, and this gentleman himself told the doctor that he had noticed the man's strange behaviour. He would at times sit down and write 50 or 60 sheets of manuscript about low women, for whom he professed to have a great hatred. Shortly before the body was found in Pinchin-street last week the man disappeared, leaving behind him the articles already mentioned, together with a packet of manuscript, which the doctor said was in exactly the same handwriting as the Jack the Ripper letters which were sent to the police. He had stated previously that he was going abroad, but a very few days before the body was discovered (Sept. 10) he was seen in the neighbourhood of Pinchin-street. The doctor is certain that this man is the Whitechapel murderer, and says that two days at the utmost will see him in custody. 'I know for a fact,' said the doctor, 'that this man is suffering from a violent form of religious mania, which attacks him and passes off at intervals. I am certain that there is another man in it besides the one I am after, but my reasons for that I cannot state. The police will have nothing to do with the capture. I am making arrangements to station six men round the spot where I know my man is, and he will be trapped.'

Chief Inspector Swanson visited Forbes Winslow who said he had been misrepresented by the *Herald*:

He produced a pair of felt galoshed boots such as are in common use in Canada, and an old coat. The felt boots were motheaten, and the slough of the moth worm remained on one of them. He then stated that the information which he relied upon was as follows:- Related by Mr. E Callaghan of 20 Gainsborough Square, Victoria Park, on Augt. 8th 1889.

'In April 1888, my wife and myself were residing at 27 Sun Street, Finsbury Square, the upper part of our house was let off to various gentlemen. In answer to our advt: we put in Daily Telegraph a Mr. G. Wentworth Bell Smith, whose business was to raise money for the Toronto Trust Society; applied and took a large bed['room' - deleted] sitting room. He said that he was over here on business and that he might stay a few months or perhaps twelve. He told us that before he had come to us he had an office at Godliman Street at the back of St Pauls. Whilst at home he occupied himself in writing on religious subjects; sometimes as many as 60 sheets of foolscap were filled up with such material. Whenever he went out of doors he would wear a different suit of clothes to what he did the day before. He had many suits of clothes and quite eight or nine hats. He kept very late hours and whenever he came in it was quite noiseless. He had also a pair of India rubber boots to put over his ordinary ones to deaden any possible sound. On Augt 9th (altered to 7th) the date of one of the murders, Mrs Callaghan was in the country, and her sister kept house in her absence.

DETECTIVE INSPECTOR EDMUND REID.

1. Detective Inspector Edmund Reid in 1887. (*Toby*)

2. Reid was popular in the press. Here he is shown astride a donkey representing Scotland Yard. (*Toby*)

3. Home Secretary Henry Matthews. (Authors' collection)

4. Commissioner Sir Charles Warren in retirement. (Authors' collection)

. Assistant Commissioner James Monro.
Authors' collection)

6. Assistant Commissioner Dr Robert
Anderson. (Authors' collection)

Superintendent Thomas Arnold.
Metropolitan Police)

8. Chief Inspector Donald Swanson.
(Metropolitan Police)

9. Detective Inspector Frederick Abberline. (*Toby*)

10. Whitechapel CID. Reid in front row, third from right. (Metropolitan Police)

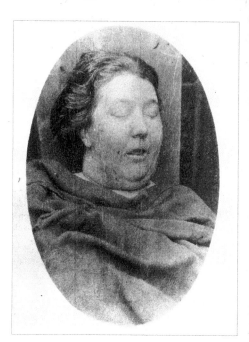

11. Martha Tabram.
(Authors' collection)

12. The Tower of London. (Authors' collection)

13. Reid in 1888. (*Illustrated Police News*)

14. Yard at rear of 29 Hanbury Street. (Authors' collection)

15. Church passage, Aldgate, looking towards murder site. (Robin Odell)

16. Reid attending Elizabeth Stride's inquest. (*Penny Illustrated Paper*)

17. Church Passage, Aldgate, from Mitre Square. (Robin Odell)

18. George Hutchinson observing Mary Kelly and a client on the night of her murder. (Authors' collection)

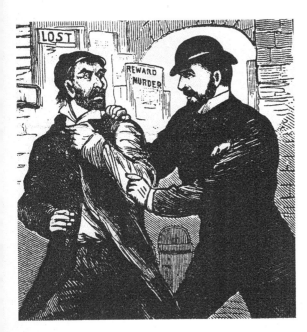

19. Arrest of a Jewish suspect. (Authors' collection)

LOCALITY OF THE SEVEN UNDISCOVERED MURDERS.

The above chart represents the locality within which, since April last, seven women of the unfortunate class have been murdered. The precise spot where each crime was committed is indicated by a dagger and a numeral.

1. April 3.—Emma Elizabeth Smith, forty-one, had a stake or iron instrument thrust through her body, near Osborn-street, Whitechapel.

2. Aug. 7.—Martha Tabram, thirty-five, stabbed in thirty-nine places, at George-yard-buildings, Commercial-street, Spitalfields.

3. Aug. 31.—Mary Ann Nicholls, forty-seven, had her throat cut and body mutilated, in Buck's-row, Whitechapel.

4. Sept. 8.—Annie Chapman, forty-seven, her throat cut and body mutilated, in Hanbury-street, Spitalfields.

5. Sept. 30.—A woman, supposed to be Elizabeth Stride, but not yet identified, discovered with her throat cut, in Berner-street, Whitechapel.

6. Sept 30.—A woman, unknown, found with her throat cut and body mutilated, in Mitre-square, Aldgate.

Figure 7 (encircled) marks the spot in Goulston-street where a portion of an apron belonging to the woman murdered in Mitre-square was picked up by a Metropolitan police-constable.

Figure 8. Nov. 9.—Mary Jane Kelly, 24, her throat cut and body terribly mutilated, in Miller's-court, Dorset-street.

20. Map showing the locations of the Whitechapel murders. (Authors' collection)

21. Sergeant Stephen White.
(*Lloyd's Weekly Newspaper*)

Above: 22. PC William Pennett who discovered the Pinchin Street Torso. (Authors' collection)

Right: 23. Reid and Sergeant William Thick at the time of Alice McKenzie's murder. (*Illustrated Police News*)

Above: 24. Inspector William Nixon Race. (*Police Review*)

Left: 25. James Thomas Sadler. (Authors' collection)

26. Chief Constable Sir Melville Macnaghten. (Metropolitan Police)

27. Reid's son-in-law Sergeant Thomas Smith, Whitechapel Division. (Metropolitan Police)

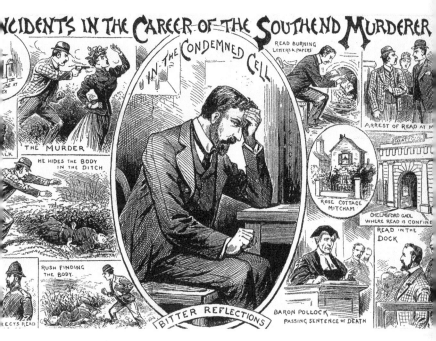

28. John Canham Read, the Southend murderer. (*Illustrated Police News*)

29. Detective Inspector Edmund Reid, 1896. (*Police Review and Parade Gossip*)

THE ACCUSED MAN, GEORGE CHAPMAN.
(From a photograph taken by the deceased woman, Maud Marsh.)

30. Severin Klosowski, alias George Chapman, the Borough poisoner. (*Shurey's Illustrated*)

31. Dr Thomas Neill Cream, the Lambeth poisoner. (Authors' collection)

32. The Lower Red Lion, Herne. (Harold Gough)

Left: 33. Reid's Ranch with its owner standing at the gate. (Harold Gough)

Above: 34. The Hampton-on-Sea Hotel. Reid in retirement selling postcards and lemonade. (Harold Gough)

35. Reid frequently aired his views in national and local newspapers. (*Lloyd's Weekly News*)

36. George Joseph Smith, the Brides in the Bath murderer. (Authors' collection)

37. Reid on the bridge over the 'Lavender Brook'. (Harold Gough)

38. Summer concerts at Herne Bay. (Authors' collection)

39. Reid examines the effects of coastal erosion on Hampton-on-Sea. (Authors' collection)

40. Sign erected by Reid at the site of Hampton Village pump. (Authors' collection)

41. Contemporary information board at Hampton-on-Sea featuring Reid. (Authors' collection)

she was however expected home that evening and we sat up for her till 4.a.m. at which hour Mr Bell Smith returned stating that he had had his watch stolen in Bishopsgate Street, which on investigation proved to be false. Shirts were found hanging on his towel horse he having washed them himself, and marks of blood on the bed. This I saw myself. Two or three days after this murder of Augt. 9th, with the stated reason of returning to Toronto. I however found that he had not done so, but he did not return to my house. He was seen getting into a tramcar in Septr. of 1888. We all regarded him as a lunatic and with delusions regarding 'Women of the streets,' who he frequently said ought to be all drowned. He told me that he was greatly impressed with the amount of immorality in London; and said that a number of whores walked up and down St. Pauls Cathedral during the service. He also said that women in the East End especially ought to be drowned. I gave this information to the police in August after the man left my house, and curiously enough the detectives came over to my house to make enquiries also about this same man, at the instigation of a lady from the Surrey side of the water. The writing of Bell Smith is in every way similar to that sent to the Police & signed Jack the Ripper. I am positive that he is the man. He is about 5ft 10in in height walks very peculiarly with his feet wide apart, knees weak and rather bending in, hair dark, complexion the same, moustache and beard closely cut giving the idea of being unshaven, nice looking teeth probably false, he appeared well conducted, was well dressed and resembled a foreigner speaking several languages entertains strong religious delusions about women, and stated that he had done some wonderful operations. His manner and habits were peculiar. Without doubt this man is the perpetrator of these crimes.'

CHAPTER FOURTEEN

The Last Whitechapel Murder

> 'He completely beat me and every police officer in London; and I have no more idea now where he lived than I had twenty years ago.'
>
> Commissioner Henry Smith, City Police

In 1890 Scotland Yard moved to the new building on the Embankment and adopted the new name, New Scotland Yard. Monro had resigned as Commissioner the same year and was succeeded by the one-armed Sir Edward Bradford.[1]

The final murder amongst the Whitechapel Murders files was that of Frances Coles (also called Coleman), on the morning of Friday 13 February 1891. This particular case is of great interest, as it was the last murder to be looked upon by both police and press as a possible Ripper killing—and, most notably, for the fact that the police felt that they had at last arrested the Whitechapel murderer.

About 2.15 a.m. on 13 February, PC 240H Ernest Thompson, a young police constable, was approaching Swallow Gardens along Chamber Street when he heard footsteps, apparently of a man, proceeding in the opposite direction towards Mansell Street. He turned left into Swallow Gardens, a passage under the railway arches off Chamber Street, leading through to Royal Mint Street, and discovered Coles lying on the ground with blood issuing from a wound in her throat. Thinking that she was still alive, for he noticed an eye movement, Thompson remained with the woman and blew his whistle for assistance. He was quickly joined by Sergeant 101H Hyde and PC 275H Hinton. Chief Inspector Swanson soon attended the scene and collected a sample of Coles' spilt blood.[2] Dr

Bagster Phillips arrived and felt that in view of the 'nature of the wound, the posture, and appearances', this was not another Ripper victim.

Inspector Reid,

in charge of a large force of police, made a house-to-house search of the district, with no result. The common lodging-houses, which abound in the district, coffee-shops, hotels, &c., were all searched, but nothing suspicious was discovered. Mr. Reid will visit the London hospitals, in order to discover when the deceased had the old wound on her head attended to, and what name she went under.

Reid made a statement to the press about his initial investigations:

In my opinion the crime has been done by the same hand that has perpetrated the other murders. We have as yet no definite clue, but hope soon to lay our hands on the fiend. I was immediately informed of the discovery, and proceeded to the spot, taking care that all approaches were blocked. The passage is well known to the police as a resort of bad women.[3]

The file cover on the murder bears some annotations, notably by Dr Anderson:

Subject Murder

Body of a woman found in Swallow Gardens with her throat cut Sir E. Bradford to see. The case was reported to me in the middle of the night & I gave authority to send Supt Arnold all the aid he might require. The officers engaged in investigating the former Whitechapel murders were early on the spot, & every effort is making to trace the criminal. But as in former cases he left nothing, & carried away nothing in the nature of property, to afford a clew

RA 3/2/1

Seen & I have shown this to Mr Matthews & explained that I think it would be premature for us to venture taking opinion as to now for this case may obviously not be connected with any previous cases.

GRL/S

13/2.

As in former cases I wish to have a report each morning for the present.

RA

13/2

On the day of the murder Albert Bachert, a prominent member of the old Whitechapel Vigilance Committee, wrote to the editor of the *Daily Chronicle*, expressing his opinion that Coles was not a victim of Jack the Ripper:

> The woman who has been murdered was seen by a friend and myself last night at a quarter past twelve outside Leman-street Railway Station speaking to a man, and when I arrived home (only a few yards from the scene of the murder), it being then five minutes past one the same woman was talking to a man opposite my house. I went inside, and later heard some loud talking. I looked out of the window, and heard the man say, 'Well, you won't come home with me?' She made some reply which I did not understand. He then said, 'If you don't you will never go home with another man.' They then walked in the direction of the arches in Chamber's-street [sic]. I have been called upon to serve on the jury to-morrow afternoon, and it is my intention to inquire into this case. If evidence is brought forward which can prove that it has been committed by the late Whitechapel fiend, I shall at once re-form the Vigilance Committee and appeal to the public for aid.[4]

At noon on Thursday 14 February, Sergeant John Don and PC Gill of H Division were in Upper East Smithfield making inquiries; they went to The Phoenix Public House, where they saw James Thomas Sadler. Sgt Don called Sadler outside the pub and confirmed his identity. Don told him that it was necessary for him to go to Leman Street Police Station, as a woman had been found with her throat cut and it was alleged that Sadler had been seen in her company the previous night. Sadler stopped Don, saying, 'I expected this.' He went with the officers and on the way to the station said:

> I am a married man and this will part me and my wife, you know what sailors are, I used her for my purpose for I have known Frances for some years. I admit I was with her, but I have a clean bill of health and can account for my time. I have not disguised myself in any way, and if you could not find me the detectives in London are no damned good. I bought the hat she was wearing and she pinned the old one under her dress. I had a row with her because she saw me knocked about and I think it was through her.

At the station Sadler was handed over to Chief Inspector Swanson, who personally took a statement from him. The importance that the police attached to this prisoner is shown by the fact that Swanson himself conducted the interview. Did they have the Jack the Ripper in custody at last? It appears that the police thought so. Sadler knew Whitechapel intimately having lived there in the late 1870s when he worked in a factory in Buck's Row. Both his wife and mother admitted he possessed a violent temper that could make him behave like a maniac, particularly when drunk.[5]

The *Daily Telegraph* reported:

It was yesterday proved that the Treasury authorities attach the greatest importance to the arrest of the ship's fireman, Sadler, who is in custody for the murder of Frances Coles, in Swallow-gardens, on Friday morning last. At the resumed inquest Mr. Charles Mathews, instructed by Mr. Pollard, was present to examine the witnesses, with the permission of the Coroner, Mr. Wynne Baxter, who whilst assenting to the arrangement, seemed impressed with its unprecedented character. Further, it is certain that the police are not neglecting the facts which came to light in connection with the previous murders. Probably the only trustworthy description of the assassin was that given by a gentleman who, on the night of the Mitre-square murder, noticed in Duke-street, Aldgate, a couple standing under the lamp at the corner of the passage leading to Mitre-square. The woman was identified as one victim of that night, Sept. 30, the other having been killed half an hour previously in Berner-street. The man was described as 'aged from thirty to thirty-five; height 5ft 7in, with brown hair and big moustache; dressed respectably. Wore pea jacket, muffler, and a cloth cap with a peak of the same material.' The witness has confronted Sadler but has failed to identify him.[6]

This report indicates that Joseph Lawende, the witness referred to, had been used in an attempt to identify Sadler as the murderer in the 1888 series of killings. Abberline did not consider Lawende a good witness in 1888. In 1891 any identification he may have made would have been worthless. The police appeared desperate to gain evidence of Sadler's guilt, for they felt they had at last captured the Whitechapel murderer. Extensive inquiries were made, witnesses as to his movements on the night of the murder were located, but nothing could be adduced to positively link him with Coles' murder. Moreover, when the police checked on his past history in an attempt to link him with the previous murders, it was found that he was at sea on several of the crucial dates, namely for the murders of Nichols, Chapman, Stride and Eddowes.[7] Eventually, they reluctantly had to release him.

The Coles inquest was opened at the Working Lads' Institute on the Saturday afternoon, presided over by Wynne Baxter. It was his eleventh inquest of the day, and to make things worse Bachert kept his promise and questioned the coroner. Baxter originally rejected Bachert as a jury member.

'You know I will inquire into the case,' Bachert retorted; 'that's why you refuse me. I am a ratepayer, and pay my rates.'

'Why should you be so anxious to serve?' Baxter asked. 'I decline to accept you.'

Bachert would not let the matter rest. After the jury had viewed the body of Coles, he again asked on what grounds Baxter refused his services.

'You be quiet, sir,' Baxter replied; 'if you are not I shall have you ejected.'

'That settles his little game,' a juryman remarked.[8]

That the Whitechapel murders still held the power to excite both press and public interest was in no doubt. Even worse, the inquest had claimed another 'victim'. One of the witnesses at the inquest was one Charles Guiver, thirty-four years old, who had viewed the body of Frances Coles and subsequently complained of headaches. After giving evidence he spent much of his time in bed asleep and on Wednesday 25 February, he fell out of bed, 'apparently in a fit.' He died that day and the post-mortem examination revealed a blood clot pressing on his brain. All his other organs were healthy and the cause of death was given as the bursting of a blood vessel in the brain, 'very likely due to excitement.'[9]

The Working Lads' Institute, the scene of so many of Wynne Baxter's dramatic inquests, had again been the focus of unwelcome public attention:

For two or three years past Mr. Baxter, the East London coroner, has always held the inquests on the bodies of persons dying suddenly in Whitechapel at the Working Lads' Institute, but since the inquiry on Frances Coles, the victim of the last Whitechapel tragedy, the authorities of the institution have refused to allow their building to be used for inquests. This, it would seem, arose from the unseemly conduct of some of the public on that occasion, and also from the fact that the hall was found extremely dirty after each day's proceedings. This determination has placed Mr. Baxter in an awkward position, as it is very difficult to obtain another suitable court in the neighbourhood.[10]

Great excitement and public reaction also marked Frances Coles' funeral. An estimated 20,000 mourners lined the funeral route all the way to the cemetery. The coffin was lowered into the ground and the Rev D. Thomas offered a prayer imploring 'God to bring to the bar of justice the cruel hand that smote the death-blow' and that the 'voice which cries from the ground for vengeance, may be heard and answered.' The murdered woman's father, in tears and enfeebled, was led away to the carriage in waiting and was spared seeing the crowd surge over the ropes and almost throw two attendant policemen into the open grave.[11]

Soon after the funeral of Frances Coles, Reid's widowed mother Martha was admitted to St Pancras Workhouse. She stayed there from 3 March until 20 May when she discharged herself.[12] It is not clear why she did not prevail upon the support of her children rather than turn to the Board of Guardians but her daughter Flora was present when she died of bronchitis on 23 November 1891, at 68 Tonbridge Street, Grays Inn Lane.

Sadler was later tracked down by the press to a dingy lodging house in Shadwell. He was suffering from bronchitis which he attributed to his time in custody. Not surprisingly he denied any knowledge of the murder of Coles whom he professed to having been on the friendliest of terms with. When asked about the other Whitechapel murders Sadler replied, 'I don't think there's a man in London who can read, who knows less about those other murders than I do.'[13]

The Whitechapel murders had ended, but they remained unsolved. At least one hundred men had been taken to police stations to be questioned for carrying black bags, having foreign accents, accosting women, or talking about Jack the Ripper in pubs. All were released after proving their identity. Eight of the eleven Whitechapel murders had taken place in Reid's H Division. He was on holiday at the time of the Chapman murder but was present for the other seven.

CHAPTER FIFTEEN

Druids and Coiners

> 'The master coiner is a cunning, secret creature, who often pursues his nefarious calling for years and years without detection.'
>
> Major Arthur Griffiths

Off duty Reid was involved in the order of Druids and was the holder of the Druids' gold medal. He was a member of the Prince Bismarck Lodge, whose meetings were held at Togo Otto Damm's White Hart Hotel in Leman Street, Whitechapel. In 1891 the Lodge unanimously agreed to form a new order, totally distinct from the Ancient Order it had previously represented. A packed meeting proposed that Brother Edmund Reid should be made 'Grand Noble Arch of the New Order into which position he was unanimously carried.' The New Order named itself 'Lodge No. 1', but the old name of Prince Bismarck stuck in the people's minds. Lodge No. 1 set out their aims. They would 'help the needy, support the sick, and provide a sum of money at any brother's death.'[1]

The social aspects of the Lodge were as important as its charitable work. At the first annual dinner, which Reid chaired, he amused the crowd of sixty members by producing a menu that had been 'prepared in a novel manner, being written in 'German-English.' The concluding information in this well-got-up card was that 'Plece Hamberlance' would be in attendance; and if that useful and compulsory means of conveyance was in the vicinity, it is believed, on this occasion its services were not required.' Members such as piano-playing Herr Schneider, baritone singer Brother Muscovitch, and conjuror Brother White regularly supplied entertainment.[2] Reid may have provided some entertainment himself at similar druidical gatherings. He was reputed to be a talented actor, singer and a skilful conjuror.[3]

A spate of arrests of forgers by Reid, in Whitechapel, culminated in the capture of the 'King of the Coiners'. It began in October 1893 when Hudson Weatherburn and Harris Marks were charged with possession of four counterfeit half-crowns and Harry 'Mad Sailor' Clements (alias Goldsmith), John 'Narky' Fieldman, and Philip 'Monkey' Cohen were charged with knowingly uttering counterfeit money in different parts of the metropolis over the previous two months.[4]

Soon afterwards labourer James Richards and laundress Ann Onley were found guilty at the Central Criminal Court of being in possession of moulds and other implements used for forging coins. They were based in Brick Lane, Whitechapel, and were caught red-handed by the police, who found fourteen newly made sixpences on the mantelpiece. Onley grabbed a mould and smashed it, crying out, 'I am not a proper maker, I have only just started the game,' but it was later found that she had a previous conviction and was sentenced to twelve months' hard labour. Richards received five years' penal servitude.[5]

Percy Miller, a crippled shoe-black, who worked outside St Mary's Station in Whitechapel, became acquainted with teenagers Cornelius Parr and Henry Bloomfield. Parr, whom Miller had known by sight, having seen him and Bloomfield in the area with a man known locally as 'Piggy', approached Miller and said, 'Here, crutchey, I have got a couple of half-crowns, and you are a shoeblack, I know you won't have a tanner [sixpence] on your stand to-day; if you take these coins and change them, I will give you a tanner on each.'

Miller took a half-crown, then made the excuse that 'I am going to the station to make water and will return shortly.' He then took the coin to Richard Griffin, the station cashier, who tested it and broke it. Miller then gave the broken coin to PC Edward Mills, who arrested Parr and Bloomfield. While in custody Bloomfield broke down in tears before DC William Thompson and said that

> I was never in such a place as this. I got it [the counterfeit coin] from a man named Smith at a coffee house in Whitechapel Road next to St Mary's Railway Station. Smith and a man named Old Steve, with one arm, met us at Smith's house of a night. Steve don't live there; he lives somewhere the other side of the water; I don't know where; Smith takes them to the coffee house and sells them.

The pair were charged by Reid with employing Miller to utter counter-feit coins. Parr received one month's imprisonment without hard labour. Bloomfield was recommended mercy by the jury and was discharged on recognizances. Next came the arrest of Charles and Annie Smith de Court, who were charged with possession of counterfeit coins with intention to utter. PC Albert Spencely made the arrest:

> On December 5th I went with Sergeant Glennester to 24 Denmark Street, St. George's-in-the-East, to the first-floor front room—I knocked, and a woman said, 'Who is there?'—Sergeant Glennester said, 'The Police'—she did not open the door, and we burst it open, and entered the room—the ser-geant said he should take her in custody for having implements for making counterfeit coin in her possession, also for uttering—she said, 'We have no money here'—the sergeant then went out of the room, and she said, 'I will tell you all the money I have here,' and got under the bed, and produced nine counterfeit half-crowns, wrapped up in a piece of newspaper, and touching each other, only there was a white powder between them—she said, 'The other things you will find, some in the drawer of the washstand, and some on the table; we should not have been in trouble if it had not been for a man named Steve.'

The de Courts were taken before the magistrate; in their defence they stated that a man called Old Steve left the things with them to mind, but that they knew nothing about them and got rid of them as soon as they could. Charles Smith de Court was found not guilty. Annie Smith de Court received six months' hard labour.[6]

Appearing in court on the same say on charges of selling thirty-two counterfeit half-crowns and thirty counterfeit florins was a man who had spent over twenty-one of his fifty-two years in prison. He was Thomas Riley, alias Stephen King, alias Old Steve, alias 'One Arm Steve the King of the Coiners'.[7] Despite having only one arm, Riley was an exceptional counterfeiter. He had 'a full coiner's machinery' in Tabard Street, which produced coins of such quality that it was extremely difficult to detect them. Riley had a gang that worked in groups of three to pass his coun-terfeit coins. They targeted post offices in the City. One of the gang would assess the possibilities; the second would distract the clerk while the third would obtain postal orders using the counterfeit coins.[8]

Reid eventually discovered Riley's base and arrested him. Riley claimed to be a French polisher who was physically incapable of being a coiner.

Two men who were serving prison sentences for passing false coins, however, testified that they used to buy counterfeit half-crowns from Riley for 4d. each and that the transaction usually took place under railway arches or down dark thoroughfares. Reid told the court that over fifty people had been arrested and sentenced after receiving coins from Riley. He was sentenced to fourteen years' penal servitude.[9]

CHAPTER SIXTEEN

Retirements and Suspects

'. . . we were almost lost in theories; there were so many of them.'
Chief Inspector Frederick Abberline

Two of the key investigators in the Whitechapel murders case retired in 1892 and 1893. Inspector Frederick Abberline 'almost broke down under the pressure.' After spending the days directing the investigation in 1888, he would spend the nights wandering the streets until 5 a.m., and 'just as he was going to bed, he would be summoned back to the East End by telegraph, there to interrogate some lunatic or suspected person whom the inspector in charge would not take the responsibility of questioning.' Abberline felt that Mary Kelly had been the last Ripper victim but at that time had no idea as to the identity of the murderer.[1] He retired in June 1892 and had a testimonial at The Three Nuns Hotel, where he was presented with 'a very handsome tea and coffee service, which was the outcome of the high estimation in which he was held by all in East London.'[2] Abberline became a private enquiry agent before working for the European Agency of the Pinkerton Detective Agency. This new role included security work at the Monte Carlo Casino, a far cry from the mean streets of East London.

Also present at this testimonial was his old boss, Superintendent Thomas Arnold of H Division, who told the gathering that

> For several years Mr Abberline had served under him in the H Division, and he assured them that he had found no better officer in the service. In losing him he felt that he was losing his right hand, and that he would have

the utmost difficulty replacing him. He felt bound to tell them, however, that when he was in trouble—as he was during the continuance of the Whitechapel crimes—Mr Abberline came down to the East End and gave the whole of his time with object of bringing these crimes to light. Unfortunately, however, the circumstances were such that success was impossible, but he could assure them that it was through no fault of Mr Abberline's that they did not succeed.[3]

Superintendent Arnold, who retired shortly after Abberline, was of the opinion that only four of the Whitechapel murders were committed by Jack the Ripper.[4] He had served in the force for thirty-six years, eighteen years as Superintendent of H Division. At Arnold's testimonial, held at The Holborn Restaurant, the chairman said that

during late years a cloud had hung over part of East London—Whitechapel— a cloud which cast horror and dismay not only on all the people of East London, but also he might say upon the whole of the civilised world. They knew the anxiety that he must have suffered, and how arduous must have been the work which he did trying to solve the mystery.

Arnold freely admitted that his division had not succeeded in 'discovering the villain.' He would have retired earlier but 'remained a few years later in the hope of solving the mystery. However they did not succeed, and if they had he would have been retiring in a much better frame of mind than he did now. Anyhow, they all did their best and no one could do any more.' Arnold received a purse containing a cheque for 500 guineas.[5]

Melville Macnaghten had joined the Metropolitan Police as assistant chief constable in June 1889 and acted as confidential assistant to the assistant commissioner of C.I.D. (Anderson).[6] Charles Warren had vetoed Macnaghten's appointment in February 1888, as he had no police or military experience. However, when he did take up the position Macnaghten impressed Monro who wrote, 'I always had a high opinion of his qualifications and abilities, but he has shown an aptitude for dealing with criminal administration and a power of managing and dealing with men for which I was not prepared; he has been doing Mr Williamsons' work for months, and he has done it with remarkable efficiency and success.'[7] Much to his chagrin, Macnaghten was not involved with the investigation of most of the Whitechapel murders but he maintained a keen interest in the crimes and kept photographs of the victims in his office safe which he showed to visitors. In 1890 Macnaghten was promoted to chief constable. The following year events would take place that led him to reveal the names of three of Scotland Yard's Jack the Ripper suspects.

On 5 March 1891 a mentally disturbed 27-year-old clerk, Thomas Hayne Cutbush, was arrested for a series of attacks on young women in Kennington and Clapham Roads. Cutbush was of slight build and very thin with a sallow complexion. He was charged with stabbing several young women after which attacks he ran off at great speed. In charge of the case was Inspector William Nixon Race of Lambeth [L] Division. The police searched his rooms and found clothes punctured and bloodstained, a Bowie knife with a six inch blade and black handle with pearl tip bearing a firm's name with a Minories address and a knife sheath which he had sewn into a hip pocket. Hidden up the chimney were waistcoats and overcoats washed in turpentine, portions of letters written in red ink, torn pieces of two rough drawings in red ink on cardboard showing two women: one a torso with the intestines exposed and the other in 'a gross attitude.'[8]

Cutbush was initially detained in Lambeth Workhouse asylum as a pauper lunatic but escaped later the same day, virtually naked, after knocking down four men and scaling an eight foot wall dressed only in a shirt. He entered a private house and stole some trousers, overcoat, hat and boots. He then returned to his home where he was rearrested. When brought up for trial at the County of London Sessions in April 1891, the jury sworn to try his mental state found him to be insane, and not capable of pleading. He was detained 'during Her Majesty's pleasure' in Broadmoor Asylum for the criminally insane.

Also arrested and indicted the previous month, in connection with similar crimes, was one Edwin Colocitt and he was ultimately discharged. He was found guilty but on sentencing his lawyer reminded the jury there was 'a case, now being investigated, in which another person was charged with the commission of exactly similar offences in the same neighbourhood and in view of the fact that the defence of the prisoner at his trial was that a mistake had been made as to his identification' which resulted in Colocitt's sentencing being postponed. His family put up a sureties and he was discharged under a promise of constant supervision.[9]

Inspector Race entertained the idea that Thomas Cutbush was one and the same person as the unknown Jack the Ripper of 1888 infamy. In fact this idea so consumed Race that he persisted in trying to convince his superior officers that he was actually responsible for the incarceration of

Jack the Ripper. Race's obsession was to have an adverse effect on his career and led to the penning of a report by Chief Constable Melville Macnaghten, now famously known as 'the Macnaghten Memorandum.' In February 1894 a series of articles were published in the *Sun* newspaper alleging that Cutbush was none other than the notorious Jack the Ripper.[10] The *Sun* luridly described Cutbush as '33 years of age, 5 foot 8 inches to 5 foot 9 inches, thin, slight stoop. Face narrow, short, high receding forehead. Eyes large and dark. Nose thick and prominent, lips full and red. Ambidextrous.' Shambling and mute, with vacuous glassy eyes, he had degenerated into degrading and disgusting habits. In March 1891 Cutbush's activities certainly would have made him an obvious Ripper 'candidate' and it is easy to see how Race came to this conclusion. The only way that the *Sun* could have made the Cutbush/Ripper connection would have been through Race, and a police officer should not disclose information that he has in his official capacity to the press.[11]

Race appears to have been a man frustrated by his own senior officers, and the *Morning Leader* published a very enlightening interview with 'a Scotland Yard Officer', surely Race, in an article headed "Jack the Ripper' Is He In The Dartmoor Prison Asylum?' [an obvious error which should read 'Broadmoor' and not 'Dartmoor'].

'I have watched the movements of this man for three years [i.e. since his arrest in March 1891], and from the evidence in my possession I hope to be able to bring home to him the charges of the Whitechapel atrocities.' So spoke an inspector of the Metropolitan Police to a Morning Leader representative yesterday afternoon. At once interesting and astonishing the information was received with a smile of incredulity. In conversation, however, a theory was elaborated and a story so circumstantially told as to almost impel conviction. It is on the credit of a responsible officer of the Criminal Investigation Department that our representative details the following narrative. It would be impolite at this stage to disclose the name of the officer in question, but the amount of interest that he has evinced in the 'Jack the Ripper' case has made him conspicuous amongst the members of the force. Briefly told his investigations are as follows:

'It was while I was on duty,' said the inspector, 'in the vicinity of Whitechapel that I became acquainted with the outrages upon women that baffled the police and shocked the sensibility of London. I became a detective in more than the ordinary sense. Dates, clues, suggestions, and theories I eagerly devoured. My pertinacity was rewarded. After a time I secured evidence, in my judgment, to lay before the Scotland Yard authorities.'

'I have in my possession now, and have already submitted it for inspection to the Scotland-yard authorities, the knife with which I shall endeavour to prove the Whitechapel murders were committed.'

'Do the Scotland-yard authorities believe in your story?' 'Well,' said the inspector, after a pause, 'they believe in my story to this extent, that they have allowed me a bonus for the information I have supplied. I do not, however, rest satisfied with that. If the man whom I am prepared to name is the murderer, I wish him brought to justice so that the English mind may be cleansed for ever of the memory of "Jack the Ripper." 'You have undertaken a large order,' said our representative. 'To begin with, where is the man?'

'At the present moment he is incarcerated in the Dartmoor [sic] Asylum, and has been there continuously from the date of the last Whitechapel murder' [i.e. Frances Coles in Swallow Gardens, Whitechapel on 13 February 1891.] was the reply.

'How then do you hope to secure his arrest and conviction?' said our representative. – 'Only with the aid of the Press,' replied the officer, 'can I hope to succeed, and you will do a public service by disclosing my story, and statements so specifically made ought easily and readily to be either confirmed or contradicted.'

'Precisely. What is your evidence?' our reporter asked.

'In my possession I hold the knife, of Chinese manufacture, with which the Whitechapel crimes were perpetrated. I, at the same time, can disclose the movements of the man whom I am prepared to name, during the intervals between the murders. I am able to trace him to the asylum after the last crime, and although he is now abandoned to insanity he has yet remembrances of the past, and all his conversations and confessions are relating to the East End horrors.'

The above statement was circumstantially told to a *Morning Leader* representative by a well-placed officer in the police force whose name can be supplied, and it seems a story that calls for investigation.[12]

The *Morning Leader* followed up this original article three days later with the heading 'The 'Jack the Ripper' Story. Scotland-Yard Now Discredits It, And The Responsible Inspector Is Hesitant.' –

The Morning Leader three days ago published a story dealing with the probability of "Jack the Ripper" being in the infirmary at Dartmoor

Gaol. That story has since been enlarged upon with more or less wisdom. However, a reporter of The Morning Leader yesterday sought the opinion of Scotland-yard – or, rather, of one of the head officials – on the story as we published it.

'There is a large basis of truth in it,' said he. 'Its only defect is that it is about three years old.'

'Then you are already acquainted with it?' asked the reporter. 'Yes,' was the bland rejoinder; 'Its leading incidents are as familiar to me as the features of my 10-year-old child.'

'You have seen the knife,' interjected our representative, 'that of Chinese manufacture?' 'Yes,' was the reply; 'I have seen the Chinese knife, and I have seen many other Chinese knives that have never seen China.'

Even the original police-inspector who is said to be responsible for the story rejects the deduction which is sought to be drawn from it.

'I never said,' he declared, in reply to his interviewer, 'that I had secured the Whitechapel murderer. All, that I have endeavoured to establish has been a carefully collected chain of circumstantial evidence, pointing almost entirely in one direction, yet at the same time capable, with added information and other facts, of being diverted into other possible channels.'

'You still believe in your own story?' 'I certainly regard it as a story demanding investigation, and until my facts have been controverted I shall continue to believe in their truth.'[13]

These were sensational, not to say controversial, statements for a serving, and rather senior, police officer to make. One can understand the consternation such publicity would have caused in the upper echelons of the Metropolitan Police.

Macnaghten's report on the Ripper murders, dated 24 February 1894, was apparently intended to deflect interest from Cutbush and to indicate that there were at least three other suspects, 'any one of whom would have been more likely than Cutbush to have committed this series of murders.' The report also defined the five women thought by Macnaghten to be the only victims of Jack the Ripper. They were Nichols, Chapman, Stride, Eddowes, and Kelly.

The first suspect was:

Mr M.J. Druitt a doctor of about 41 years of age & of fairly good family, who disappeared at the time of the Miller's Court murder, and whose body was found floating in the Thames on 31st Dec: i.e. 7 weeks after the said murder. The body was said to have been in the water for a month, or more – on it was found a season ticket between Blackheath & London. From private information I have little doubt but that his own family suspected this man of being the Whitechapel murderer; it was alleged that he was sexually insane.

Montague John Druitt was in fact a barrister and schoolteacher aged thirty-one years. He had been dismissed from his teaching post in late November 1888 after 'he had got in serious trouble.' Despite statements to the contrary, Druitt was a fairly successful barrister and was still arguing cases in court until shortly before his death.[14] He was the son of a surgeon and his mother was the inmate of an asylum at the time of the murders. It is clear that Macnaghten favoured Druitt as the most likely of the three to have been the Ripper. His evidence for this is not known, but he hypothesised that 'the murderer's brain gave way altogether after his awful glut in Miller's Court, and that he immediately committed suicide.'

The source of Macnaghten's enigmatic reference to 'private information' was hinted at in an article in the *Bristol Times* and *Mirror*:

I give a curious story for what it is worth. There is a West of England member [of Parliament] who in private declares that he has solved the mystery of 'Jack the Ripper.' His theory—and he repeats it with so much emphasis that it might also be called his doctrine—is that 'Jack the Ripper' committed suicide on the night of his last murder. I can't give details, for fear of a libel action; but the story is so circumstantial that a good many people believe it. He states that a man with blood-stained clothes committed suicide on the night of the last murder, and he asserts that the man was the son of a surgeon, who suffered from homicidal mania. I do not know what the police think of the story, but I believe that before long a clean breast will be made, and that the accusation will be sifted thoroughly.[15]

An article appeared in the *Western Mail* the following year enlarging on this report and stating that the MP was a Mr. Farquharson who represented West Dorset constituency which covered Wimborne, the home town of the Druitt family.[16] This story undoubtedly would have been brought to the attention of Macnaghten who later wrote that 'I have destroyed all my documents and there is now no record of the secret information which came into my possession.'[17]

The second suspect was:

> Kosminski, a Polish Jew, & resident in Whitechapel. This man became insane owing to many years indulgence in solitary vices. He had a great hatred of women, specially of the prostitute class, & had strong homicidal tendencies; he was removed to a lunatic asylum about March 1889. There were many circumstances connected with this man which made him a strong suspect.

Research has indicated that the only person named Kosminski who had been put into an asylum was Aaron Kosminski, who was sent to Colney Hatch asylum in February 1891.[18] This took place eight days before the murder of Frances Coles which many believed at the time to be another Ripper killing. Kosminski's case notes describe him as an unmarried hairdresser. They show that 'He declares that he is guided and altogether controlled by an instinct that informs his mind; he says that he knows the movements of all mankind; he refuses food from others because he is told to do so and eats out of the gutter for the same reason. He took up a knife and threatened the life of his sister.' He was apathetic and melancholic although once he became 'excited & violent—a few days ago he took up a chair, and attempted to strike the charge attendant.'[19] He was transferred to Leavesden asylum for imbeciles in Hertfordshire in 1894 and died there in 1919 from gangrene of the left leg. There is nothing in his surviving asylum case files to suggest he was suspected of being Jack the Ripper. Aaron Kosminski's only known criminal conviction was for walking an unmuzzled dog in December 1889, a full year after the murders. He claimed the dog was not his but still received a ten shilling fine at the magistrates' court.[20]

The third suspect was:

> Michael Ostrog a mad Russian doctor & a convict & unquestionably a homicidal maniac. This man was said to have been habitually cruel to women, & for a long time was known to have carried about with him surgical knives & other instruments; his antecedents were of the very worst & his whereabouts at the time of the Whitechapel murders could never be satisfactorily accounted for.

Ostrog's known criminal career in England stretched from 1863 to 1904. He was a prolific thief and confidence trickster who used over twenty different aliases but was frequently arrested and imprisoned in different parts of southern England. Alleged to have had some medical training, he was mentally unstable and occasionally violent. The *Police Gazette* contained an illustration of Ostrog, describing him as a 55-year-old Jew and that 'special attention is drawn to this dangerous man.'[21] At the time of a previous arrest he had drawn a revolver. Nothing is yet known of him after his release from prison in September 1904 (for stealing a microscope in Whitechapel).[22] However, Ostrog had been arrested in Paris on 26 July 1888 for the fraudulent removal of a microscope and convicted on 14 November. Detained in France he could not have been Jack the Ripper.

The ultimate purpose of Macnaghten's report was almost certainly to provide the chief commissioner, Sir Edward Bradford, with material to answer the Home Office should the sensational articles in the *Sun* result in an enquiry from that quarter as to the police position on the allegations. The *Sun* of 19 February 1894 did indeed indicate that newspaper's desire to have the subject further aired and one of their representative's called on the radical MP Henry Labouchere and mentioned the series of articles. Whilst Labouchere agreed that the *Sun* had made out 'a fair case for public investigation' he said that their circumstantial case fell far short of proof. In the event no public investigation was called for and the report was never used; it remained in the Metropolitan Police files where it still reposes today.

For his part Race had doomed his future police career, in the police service you simply do not 'rock the boat' and incur the displeasure of your senior officers, and the more senior those officers are the worse it is. In December 1897 he was compelled to go on sick leave, his illness apparently brought on by the loss of his 21-year-old son 'and also through being treated indifferently in the Police Force.' It was noted that despite having been recommended several times for promotion by his superintendent, which was richly deserved in view of his excellent record, 'through some unknown reason he never heard anything further, a thing almost unprecedented in the Service, and which worried him greatly . . . unfortunately after this honourable career, he was reduced without any fair trial and has now been invalided out on a small pension of 16s. 3d. per week.' Race's actual retirement date was 1 April 1898; he was forty-three years old and had seen almost eighteen years service with the Metropolitan Police Force. [23]

A fourth—and contemporary—police suspect has been identified in recent years with the discovery of the 'Littlechild letter'. Ex-Detective Chief Inspector John George Littlechild, head of the Special Branch at Scotland Yard in 1888, wrote this letter on 23 September 1913 to the famous journalist, author, and playwright, George R Sims. In the letter Littlechild stated that Dr Francis Tumblety, a 56-year-old American quack doctor, was 'amongst the suspects.' Littlechild qualified this statement by saying that to his mind Tumblety was 'a very likely one,' adding that Tumblety's 'feelings towards women were remarkable and bitter in the extreme' and that there was an as yet undiscovered 'large dossier' on Tumblety at Scotland Yard. Tumblety was known to possess a collection of women's wombs in jars.

Robert Anderson knew about Tumblety for he sent a cablegram to San Francisco's Police Chief, Patrick Crowley, who had offered Anderson samples of Tumblety's handwriting. Anderson gratefully replied, on 22 November, 'Thanks. Send handwriting and all details you can of Tumblety.'[24]

Tumblety had been arrested on charges of gross indecency in London on 7 November but escaped back to the United States despite Scotland Yard sending a detective in pursuit. In New York Tumblety was tracked down by a reporter from the New York *World*. The 'celebrated Whitechapel suspect' had the following to say about his arrest:

> I have been going over to England for a long time – ever since 1869, indeed – and I used to go about the city a great deal until every part of it became familiar to me. I happened to be there when these Whitechapel murders attracted the attention of the whole world, and in company with thousands of other people, I went down to the Whitechapel district. I was not dressed in a way to attract attention, I thought, though it afterwards turned out that I did. I was interested by the excitement and the crowds and the queer scenes and sights, and did not know that all the time I was being followed by English detectives.
>
> My guilt was very plain to the English mind. Someone had said that Jack the Ripper was an American, and everybody believed that statement. Then it is the universal belief among the lower classes that al Americans wear slouch hats: therefore, Jack the Ripper must wear a slouch hat, and this, together with the fact that I was an American, was enough for the police. It established my guilt beyond question.[25]

Another alleged suspect was William Henry Bury, who was arrested in Dundee for the murder of his wife on 10 February 1889. Suspicion had attached to him because, when his wife's body was discovered, there was writing on the wall of the house stating that 'Jack the Ripper is at the back of this door,' and 'Jack the Ripper is in this seller [sic]'.[26] At the time of the 1888 murders Bury and his wife Ellen had resided in Bow, and his wife's body had been mutilated after she had been strangled with a rope. Bury never confessed to the Ripper crimes, but his name has often since been linked with them.

James Berry, the public executioner, hanged Bury at Dundee Prison in April 1889. He recalled:

> Scotland Yard detectives had taken the case up, and, unknown to the police of Dundee were visiting every haunt of the prisoner, and submitting to a vigorous cross-examination everyone who had known him . . . it was with long weapons similar to those which Bury used in his business that the Whitechapel murders were committed . . . I have put it on record that two of his [the Commissioner of the Metropolitan Police] staff came all the way to Dundee to see the man, to keep their ears open for any confession, and afterwards to submit me to a stiff cross-examination.

As Berry walked into the condemned cell Bury said to him, 'I suppose you think you are clever to hang me.' Whilst pinioning Bury the hangman whispered, 'Now if you have anything to say it will be as well for you to say it. When I get you on the scaffold I will not give you time to unburden yourself. It is your last chance.' Bury 'never opened his mouth' and all his secrets died with him.

Berry continued:

> After the execution was over the Scotland Yard men came at once to see me. 'Well, Mr. Berry,' they said, 'will you tell what opinion you have about him?' 'Did you hear him make that statement?' I asked. 'Oh, yes, but unfortunately you could construe it in two or three ways. It is nothing definite to go on. What do you think yourself?' 'I think it is him right enough.' 'And we agree with you,' replied one of the detectives. 'We know all about his movements in the past, and we are quite satisfied that you have hanged 'Jack the Ripper.' There will be no more Whitechapel crimes.'[27]

Edmund Reid does not appear to have ever mentioned any of the above contemporary suspects and it is not clear how much he knew about them. What is clear is that he did not think any of them were Jack the Ripper for he believed that Frances Coles had been the Ripper's last victim. That murder had taken place after Druitt and Bury were dead while Kosminski was in an asylum. Moreover, Ostrog had been languishing in a French prison during the second half of 1888.

CHAPTER SEVENTEEN

Reid's Ripper Reminiscences

> 'I was at the scene and ought to know.'
>
> Edmund Reid

Edmund Reid's daughter, Elizabeth, married H Division PC (later Sergeant) Thomas Smith in 1895. Reid was transferred from H Division to L (Lambeth) Division on 9 December 1895,[1] but retired soon afterwards, on 27 February 1896.[2] He was issued with a number 3 certificate, denoting good conduct. His entry in the Metropolitan Police removal register lists him as John James Reid, with 'Edwin' being inserted afterwards. The date of joining was incorrectly recorded as '4.11.1892', rather than 4 November 1872.[3]

Reid's pension records note that he was entitled to a pension of £117 a year (his salary was £4. 7s. a week when he retired). Aged forty-nine years old, he had served twenty-three years and twenty-eight days. He was five feet six inches tall and had dark brown hair, grey eyes, a fresh complexion, and no identifying marks or defects. One newspaper reported that Reid was obliged to retire early due to ill-health.[4] The record showed that he had been injured in the service but did not specify the nature of the injury. He and his wife, Emily Jane, lived at 59b Block, Stepney Buildings, Stepney.[5] Reid had received fifty rewards and commendations and retired with 'sufficient medals for acts of bravery to cover his breast.'[6]

His departure was marked by a presentation from his colleagues at Scotland Yard, to whom he was affectionately known as 'Teddy', of a salver inscribed as follows: 'Presented to Edmund Reid, of the Criminal Investigation Department, by his brother inspectors, on his retirement from the force, February 21, 1896.'[7] After starting his career as the short-est officer in the Metropolitan Police he retired as the oldest serving detec-tive inspector.[8]

On 6 March 1896, a committee was formed at a public meeting of Whitechapel tradesmen in order to organise 'a gigantic testimonial scheme for the benefit of the genial detective.'[9] At the time of his retirement it was noted that Edmund and Emily Reid were both 'in excellent spirits and thoroughly enjoying retirement in the heart of the district of the East End where they have made quite a host of good friends.'[10]

This public renown in the East End was exemplified some time later. In 1902 Reid struck up a conversation with a 'son of Israel' in the tiny hamlet of Hampton-on-Sea on the East Kent coast. Reid 'chanced to make use of an expression known to Jews who live in Whitechapel. The Jew gave me a searching glance, then all at once blurted out, 'You're Reid?' I confessed I was. The Jew jumped up from his seat and shook hands with me most effusively. He was pleased to see me. The chat which followed was most enjoyable.'[11]

Reid looked back with fondness over his police career. It seemed to him that '. . . I had law and order instinct in me . . . there seems a fair prospect of the instinct being continued in other generations of Reids. I loved the work.'[12] Of all the cases Reid had worked on, it was the Whitechapel murders which presented him with the most difficulties and the greatest press attention. They were described as 'the most trying time of Mr. Reid's career when he and his staff had to work almost night and day for a long period.'[13] Even in his retirement at Hampton-on-Sea Reid could not forget the horror of the Whitechapel murders.

Shortly after his retirement a reporter from London's *Weekly Dispatch* tracked down the media-friendly ex-detective at his testimonial. The *Dispatch*'s representative 'grasped Mr Reid by the arm because he was an ex-detective with his tongue untied and that specialist [the reporter] was anxious to make that tongue wag a little.' Reid, 'like a good hearted fellow', agreed to an interview.

'Just sit right there,' as the Yankees of Leicester Square put it, 'and tell me a few stories,' Reid said. 'You've heard about the Scotsman who paid his railway fare twice and—'

'No, I haven't, and I don't want any fairy tales,' interrupted the reporter. 'I want you just to give me a few facts about cases you have been engaged on during your professional career.'

The conversation naturally turned to the Whitechapel murders and Reid had no qualms about admitting his failure to catch Jack the Ripper.

The *Weekly Dispatch* was uncritical. They thought that

not even Sherlock Holmes could have solved the case because the great charm of Sherlock Holmes was his reasoning power. Jack the Ripper defied reason. Reason cannot cope with mania until mania is in chains or enclosed within four walls. Otherwise we should not need lunatic asylums. Further, there are cleverer men at Scotland Yard than Sherlock Holmes to-day—and there were cleverer detectives whose best work was put into the attempt to capture Jack the Ripper between 1888 and 1892. Among these was one of the most remarkable men of the century, Edmund Reid.

It is as the chief detective inspector in charge of the Whitechapel district during the period of the Ripper murders that Mr Reid must always be an exceptionally interesting official. He had charge of the detective arrangements made with a view of capturing the murderer. As we now know, all the efforts of Reid, of the special police, and of the special staff of Scotland Yard men drafted into the district were ineffectual. No one regrets this more than Reid, and no one worked harder than he to drop upon the terrible mad creature who eluded all his pursuers. What Reid has to say about Jack the Ripper, therefore, now he has no longer any need to keep silent, is valuable. From 1888 to 1892 there were in all nine 'Ripper' murders—that is to say, nine murders covering the period which displayed the same cruel mad ferocity and the same hand. There is no doubt in Reid's mind that Jack the Ripper was a homicidal maniac, whose mania was in every instance subjective. That is to say, the Ripper never sought out or pursued his victims. In every instance the murderer had been taken by his victim to a hidden spot for immoral purposes, and there the mania came upon him, and it was the fact that the women themselves always took so much care to hide their actions, never venturing to their hiding places when any person was in sight, that was the chief secret of the police never under any circumstances being able to obtain the slightest clue, or slightest description of the man. Further, the Ripper always took the lives of his victims so swiftly that there never could have been a struggle or a cry from one of them. How he mutilated the bodies afterwards—the whole story of the murders is too terrible to bear description. It is gratifying to know, however, that in the opinion of detective Reid, the maniac has been dead some years. The mania was of a nature which must long ago have resulted in the death of the maniac—an opinion that is borne out by the best medical experts who have studied the case.[14]

Memories of the Ripper resurfaced in 1901 following a murder at Crossingham's Lodging House, 35 Dorset Street, Spitalfields. It led to speculation that Jack the Ripper had returned to the district and resumed his murderous spree. The victim was a 28-year-old, 'handsome, buxom, brunette,' Mary Ann Austin.[15] Austin had recently separated from her dockside labourer husband, William, after eight stormy years of marriage. She drifted around the common lodging houses after being thrown out of Miller's Court. On the last Saturday in May she told an acquaintance at The Queen pub in Commercial Street that she had met a Russian in the Commercial Road and planned to meet him that night.

Shortly before midnight Austin and a male companion arrived at Crossingham's Lodging House. The man paid 1s. 6d. for double cubicle number 15, 'a price higher than ordinary, out of consideration of the fact that it was a Saturday when the Eastender is supposed to be flush.'[16] Between 8 and 9 a.m. lodger Frances Davis informed the deputy lodging house keeper's wife, Maria Moore, that she had heard groans from cubicle 15. When Moore entered the cubicle she found a naked Mary Ann Austin 'horribly outraged'[17] and saw signs of a struggle in the cubicle. Austin was unceremoniously bundled into a cab and deposited at the London Hospital. Metropolitan Police surgeon Dr Frankland Hewett Oliver found 'no less than ten wounds in the fleshy part of the abdomen which, it was subsequently found, penetrated the wall of the peritoneal cavity.'[18] Oliver concluded that the wounds had been inflicted by 'some sharp pointed instrument, but nothing could be ascertained as to its probable length or breadth.'[19] He unsuccessfully looked for fingerprints on the body. Austin was also 'extensively bruised as to suggest she had been kicked all over the body.'[20] Before dying Austin told London Hospital's Dr Edwin Reach that she had met her attacker in the street and did not know who he was but thought he was Jewish. Maria Moore described the man who had entered Crossingham's with Austin as 'a short, dark man with a Jewish cast of feature, he had dark hair and moustache, but no side whiskers or beard. I don't know what colour his eyes were.'[21] A lodger named Bates added that the man 'had a silver ring on his left hand, wore a grey check cap, and had a red and black scarf around his neck.'[22]

The case remained unsolved, although a police informant accused a man named George Neating. Neating had told the informant that he was 'a member of the Metropolitan Police at the time of the Whitechapel murders and that when he had done anything wrong or anything had happened on his beat he would hide himself away among the tombstones in Stepney churchyard and that he was subsequently dismissed from the force through drunkenness. On the date of the murder of a woman at Spitals Court some short time ago Neating left Cardiff and is supposed to have gone to London.' There was no trace of a George Neating in the personnel records of H or K Divisions and attempts to trace him failed.[23]

Despite the passage of ten years since the Swallow Gardens murder of Frances Coles, the *Sun* sought the opinions of former Special Branch Detective Sergeant Patrick McIntyre, and Edmund Reid. McIntyre felt that there was a possibility that Austin was murdered by the Ripper, suggesting that he may have been arrested for another offence shortly after the murder of Frances Coles, for which he received a sentence of ten years' penal servitude, and recommenced his murders upon being released. He thought it would be worthwhile to conduct 'a thorough inquiry into the history of every convict who has returned home to Spitalfields after being in prison during the time the Ripper murders have ceased.'

Reid disagreed, and in a report he drew up for the *Sun*'s journalist he stated that:

The Ripper was a man with no skilled knowledge—not even the skill of a novice in butchery. In every instance the mutilation was clumsy in the extreme—was the hacking and tearing of a man in a frenzy, increasing in intensity as his work proceeded. It is said that in the case of the woman Kelly that portions of the body were carried away. This was not true. Every body was found complete [sic]. It was simply hacked without any system or plan other than dictated by ferocity. Another absurd theory was that the murders were committed by a left-handed man who had seized his victim from behind. The evidence was quite contrary to this. In the throat cutting the fiend had shown cunning. The position of the blood and the body showed that he had stood face to face with the woman, and had slashed her throat, with his right hand from right to left, causing the blood to spurt away from him, so that he probably never had any blood stains on his clothes. One of the great difficulties of the case for the police was that it was a case of a maniac's cunning outwitting reason's methods. Every murder was committed in a dark, secluded spot, generally on private property, as in the case of the woman Austin, now under investigation. As no one saw ever saw the man except his victims, not the slightest evidence could be obtained as to his description.

Reid repeated his belief that 'the man who committed the Ripper murders has long since been dead, a victim to the consuming frenzy for mutilation, a frenzy which must have long ago destroyed the man body and soul.'[24] Reid's memories, like many of those of his colleagues, were to a degree affected by the passage of time. His conclusions, however, seemed to remain unchanged. It was not the last he was to have to say on the subject.

Two years later Reid's former colleague, Frederick Abberline, had been reading newspaper reports at his Bournemouth home on the arrest and trial of George Chapman, formerly Severin Klosowski. George Chapman was born in Poland in 1865 where he worked as a barber-surgeon before arriving in Whitechapel in 1888. He took employment as a hairdresser's assistant before holding a number of positions as a hairdresser and publican. The libidinous Chapman lived with various women and deceived several into believing they were his lawfully wedded wife. Three of the women died from the effects of the poison Chapman gave them. He was eventually arrested and executed at Wandsworth in 1903.

Abberline started to make notes. Was this man his former quarry, Jack the Ripper? The retired detective intended to convey his suspicions to the assistant commissioner, Melville Macnaghten, but a fall in the garden led to an injured hand and shoulder, which prevented him from doing so. A timely visit by a *Pall Mall Gazette* reporter saved him the trouble, and he told all to the London tabloid, listing the circumstantial evidence which had helped him form his theory:

I have been so struck with the remarkable coincidences in the two series of murders that I have not been able to think of anything else for several days past . . . I cannot help feeling that this is the man we struggled so hard to capture fifteen years ago. As I say, there are a score of things which make one believe that Chapman is the man; and you must understand that we have never believed all those stories about Jack the Ripper being dead, or that he was a lunatic, or anything of that kind. For instance, the date of the arrival in England coincides with the beginning of the series of murders in Whitechapel; there is a coincidence also in the fact that the murders ceased in London when 'Chapman' went to America, while similar murders began to be perpetrated in America after he landed there. The fact that he studied medicine and surgery in Russia before he came over here is well established, and it is curious to note that the first series of murders was the work of an expert surgeon, while the recent poisoning cases were proved to be done by a man with more than an elementary knowledge of medicine. There are many other things extremely remarkable. The fact that Klosowski when he came to reside in this country occupied a lodging in George Yard, Whitechapel Road, where the first murder was committed, is very curious, and the height of the man and the peaked cap he is said to have worn quite tallies with the descriptions I got of him. All agree too that he was a foreign looking man, but that of course helped us little in a district so full of foreigners.[25]

Again we see the curious faulty recollection of a retired police officer as to the precise facts of the events of earlier years. Despite his suspicions against Chapman, Abberline held the same opinion as Reid as to the Ripper's identity. He said 'that Scotland Yard is really no wiser on the subject than it was fifteen years ago.' The reporter proposed the Lambeth Poisoner, Dr Thomas Neill Cream, as a possible suspect. Cream had been executed in November 1892 at Newgate after the murder by strychnine of several prostitutes: 'that is another idle story,' replied Mr Abberline, 'Neill Cream was not even in the country when the Whitechapel murders took place. No; the identity of the diabolical individual has yet to be established.'[26]

Coincidentally a letter appeared in London's *Morning Advertiser* from a correspondent signing himself 'Unofficial', in which he dismissed the likelihood of Cream as a suspect and then described the three suspects as outlined by Melville Macnaghten in his 1894 report. He added:

the fact remains that Scotland Yard is under the impression that the identity of 'Jack the Ripper' was known. By inquiry they had honed the issue down to one of three persons, all of whom disappeared shortly after the final horror in Miller's Court. One was a Polish Jew, who was shut up in an asylum as a homicidal lunatic. Another was an insane Russian doctor, who was an ex-convict. He, too, was put into a lunatic asylum. The third was also a doctor, in the prime of life, but insane. He disappeared directly after the last 'Ripper' tragedy, and his body was found floating in the Thames. The sudden cessation of this series of murders points to the death or confinement of 'Jack the Ripper' soon after the last murder.[27]

Reid swiftly responded to the press statements of both Abberline and 'Unofficial'. Regarding Abberline's interview, Reid believed his old colleague had been misreported:

I think I know that gentleman better than to think he could have said that the series of murders was the work of an expert surgeon, when he knew that it was nothing more than a number of slashes all over the body of the victim, even after the murderer knew his victim was dead. Again, the late Dr Phillips, police surgeon, were he alive now, would tell you that at no time was any part of the body missing [sic]. No description of Jack the Ripper was ever obtained, and to compare his work with that of Chapman is like comparing the work of a bricklayer with that of a watchmaker.[28]

Reid was obviously mistaken in the belief that no body parts were ever stolen. It may be easier to reconcile this with a faulty memory, however, for in the cases where such parts were taken—Chapman, Eddowes and, possibly, Kelly—Reid was not directly involved in the inquiry. At the time of Chapman's murder he was on leave, Eddowes was a City Police case and Kelly was handled by Abberline although Reid took part in the investigation; the question of the missing heart is still a contentious one. Reid would also appear to be of the opinion that the suspect descriptions the police had obtained were not positively of the killer.

Addressing the points raised by 'Unofficial', Reid was:

glad to see that the writer of a letter in your paper of the 25 inst., signed himself 'Unofficial' for more reason than one. I was not aware that the last horror was committed in Miller's Court. I was always under the impression that the last of the so called 'Ripper murders' was committed in Swallow Gardens [it was the last in the 'Whitechapel murders' file]. It was there that the late Police Constable Thompson heard footsteps receding but did not see anyone about the spot where he saw the body of Frances Coles on the 13th February 1891. It is certainly news to me that the last of the murders took place in 1888. I was under the impression that that was the year of the first. So that the insane doctor of whom 'Unofficial' speaks must have been a wonderful man to have committed nine murders [sic] after his body was found floating in the Thames in 1888. Again I am not aware any murder was committed in Mitre Court. There was one committed in Mitre Square, in the City, but whatever Police Constable Thompson was doing there out of Metropolitan district, one is at a loss to know. Perhaps 'Unofficial' can explain, as he appears to know all about it.[29]

Reid evidently confuses some of the facts, or is misreported, as there were not nine murders after the discovery of Druitt's body in the Thames. He must have meant that in his opinion there had been nine murders in the series (excluding Mylett and the Pinchin Street torso), some of which were committed after Druitt's suicide. Clearly 'Unofficial' was wrong in suggesting that PC Thompson was present at the scene of the 'Mitre court' murder; indeed, Thompson hadn't even joined the force at that time.

CHAPTER EIGHTEEN

Anderson's Suspect

'Anderson . . . only thought he knew.'

Chief Inspector John Littlechild

Dr Robert Anderson held a unique post as head of the C.I.D. at the time of the Whitechapel murders; his own comments on the case, therefore, are relevant and important. In 1892 Anderson was interviewed by a representative of *Cassell's Saturday Journal*. Anderson mused, 'I sometimes think myself an unfortunate man for between twelve and one [sic] on the morning of the day I took up my position here the first Whitechapel murder occurred.' The journalist continued:

> The mention of this appalling sequence of still undiscovered crimes leads to the production of certain ghastly photographs.
>
> 'There,' says the Assistant Commissioner, 'there is my answer to people who come with fads and theories about these murders. It is impossible to believe they were acts of a sane man – they were those of a maniac revelling in blood.'[1]

There do appear to be some contradictions, however, in what he had to say. In 1895 Major Arthur Griffiths, inspector of prisons and Anderson's friend wrote in the *Windsor Magazine* under the pseudonym 'Alfred Aylmer' on 'The Detective In Real Life'. He had the following to say of Anderson and the Ripper:

> Although he has achieved greater success than any detective of his time, there will always be undiscovered crimes, and just now the tale is pretty

full. Much dissatisfaction was vented upon Mr. Anderson at the utterly abortive efforts to discover the perpetrator of the Whitechapel murders. He has himself a perfectly plausible theory that Jack the Ripper was a homicidal maniac, temporarily at large, whose hideous career was cut short by committal to an asylum.[2]

In 1898 Griffiths published his book, *Mysteries of Police and Crime*, in which he listed the three Ripper suspects described by Macnaghten in his 1894 report, although the names of the three were not mentioned.

Anderson had retired and was knighted in 1901. His book, *Criminals and Crime*, was published in 1907, and in it he had this to say of the Whitechapel murders:

> Or again, take a notorious case of a different kind, 'the Whitechapel murders' of the autumn of 1888. At that time the sensation-mongers of the newspaper press fostered the belief that life in London was no longer safe, and that no woman ought to venture abroad in the streets after nightfall. And one enterprising journalist went so far as to impersonate the cause of all this terror as 'Jack the Ripper,' a name by which he will probably go down to history. But no amount of silly hysterics could alter the fact that these crimes were a cause of danger only to a particular section of a small and definite class of women, in a limited district of the East End; and that the inhabitants of the metropolis generally were just as secure during the weeks the fiend was on the prowl, as they were before the mania seized him, or after he had been safely caged in an asylum.

Anderson's views on crime were sometimes sought by the press when there was a newsworthy item of criminal interest to report. Such an occasion arose in 1908, when the Sevenoaks Luard murder case, a classic murder mystery in its own right, was in the news. A *Daily Chronicle* reporter interviewed Anderson and reported his thoughts on police investigation methods. In doing so the Whitechapel murders were again mentioned:

> In two cases of that terrible series there were distinct clues destroyed—wiped out absolutely—clues that might very easily have secured for us proof of the identity of the assassin.
>
> In one case it was a clay pipe. Before we could get to the scene of the murder the doctor had taken it up, thrown it into the fire-place and smashed it beyond recognition.

In another case there was writing in chalk on the wall—a most valuable clue; handwriting that might have been at once recognised as belonging to a certain individual. But before we could secure a copy, or get it protected, it had been entirely obliterated.[3]

The pipe referred to must have been that found in Kelly's room, as a fireplace is mentioned. That pipe was not lost, however, and was known to belong to Barnett. The pipe that was smashed related to the McKenzie murder and was used by McKenzie herself. The writing on the wall in Goulston Street was not proved at the time to be the work of the murderer, and its removal was ordered by Sir Charles Warren himself after a copy had been taken. Furthermore, in both cases the police were the first on the scene. These comments, together with what was described as a 'perfectly plausible theory', are difficult to reconcile with his soon-to-be-made assertion that the identity of the Ripper was definitely known to the Metropolitan Police.

This progression of Anderson's statements about the Whitechapel murders continued in the publication of his autobiographical book, *The Lighter Side of My Official Life*, in 1910. By now his theory as to the identity of Jack the Ripper was a fact. It was first serialised in *Blackwood's Magazine*, and there Anderson wrote:

One did not need to be a Sherlock Holmes to discover that the criminal was a sexual maniac of a virulent type; that he was living in the immediate vicinity of the scenes of the murders; and that, if he was not living absolutely alone, his people knew of his guilt, and refused to give him up to justice. During my absence abroad the Police had made a house-to-house search for him, investigating the case of every man in the district whose circumstances were such that he could go and come to get rid of his blood-stains in secret. And the conclusion we came to was that he and his people were low-class Jews, for it is a remarkable fact that people of that class in the East End will not give up one of their number to Gentile Justice.

And the result proved that our diagnosis was right on every point. For I may say at once that 'undiscovered murders' are rare in London, and the 'Jack the Ripper' crimes are not in that category.

A footnote added the following: 'the individual whom we suspected was caged in an asylum, the only person who ever had a good view of the murderer at once identified him, but when he learned that the suspect was a fellow-Jew he declined to swear to him.'[4] In his book Anderson added: 'In saying that he [the murderer] was a Polish Jew I am merely stating a definitely ascertained fact.'

In a 1912 series of articles in the *People* newspaper entitled 'Scotland Yard And Its Secrets,' by H.L. Adam, the introduction was written by Anderson, who wrote:

> and yet, even without the evidence which sent the murderer [Crippen] to the gallows, the moral proof of his guilt would have been full and clear. So again with 'the Whitechapel Murders' of 1888. Despite the lucubrations of many an amateur 'Sherlock Holmes,' there was no doubt whatever as to the identity of the criminal, and if our London 'detectives' possessed the powers, and might have recourse to the methods of foreign police forces, he would have been brought to justice. But the guilty sometimes escape through the working of a system designed to protect the innocent persons wrongly accused of crime. And many a case which is used to disparage our British 'detectives' ought rather to be hailed as a proof of the scrupulous fairness with which they discharge their duties.[5]

It seems clear that the suspect being referred to by Anderson was the one named in the Macnaghten report as Kosminski. Indeed, this was later confirmed by the discovery of marginal notes in ex-Superintendent Swanson's copy of Anderson's autobiography. Swanson wrote that the witness refused to testify, 'because the suspect was also a Jew and also because his evidence would convict the suspect, and witness would be the means of murderer being hanged which he did not wish to be left on his mind. And after this identification which suspect knew, no other murder of this kind took place in London.' On the endpaper of the book Swanson added, 'after the suspect had been identified at the Seaside Home where he had been sent by us with difficulty in order to subject him to identification, and he knew he was identified. On suspect's return to his brother's house in Whitechapel he was watched by police (City CID) by day & night. In a very short time the suspect with his hands tied behind his back, he was sent to Stepney Workhouse and then to Colney Hatch and died shortly afterwards – Kosminski was the suspect.'[6]

The *Jewish Chronicle* quickly responded to Anderson's controversial allegations. Their editor Leopold Jacob Greenberg, writing a column under the name 'Mentor', said:

Sir Robert Anderson, the late head of the Criminal Investigation Department at Scotland Yard, has been contributing to Blackwood's a series of articles on Crime and Criminals. In the course of his last contribution, Sir Robert tells his readers that the fearful crimes committed in the East End some years ago, and known as 'Jack the Ripper' crimes, were the work of a Jew. Of course, whoever was responsible for the series of foul murders was not mentally responsible, and this Sir Robert admits. But I fail to see—at least, from his article in Blackwood's—upon what evidence worthy of the name he ventures to cast the odium for this infamy upon one of our people. It will be recollected that the criminal, whoever he was, baffled the keenest search not alone on the part of the police, but on the part of an infuriated and panic-stricken populace. Notwithstanding the utmost vigilance, the man, repeating again and again his demoniacal work, again and again escaped. Scotland Yard was nonplussed, and then, according to Sir Robert Anderson, the police 'formed a theory'—usually the first essential to some blundering injustice. In this case, the police came to the conclusion that 'Jack the Ripper' was a 'low-class' Jew, and they so decided, Sir Robert says, because they believe 'it is a remarkable fact that people of that class in the East End will not give up one of their number to Gentile justice.' Was anything more nonsensical in the way of a theory ever conceived even in the brain of a policeman? Here was a whole neighbourhood, largely composed of Jews, in constant terror lest their womenfolk, whom Jewish men hold in particular regard—even 'low-class' Jews do that—should be slain by some murderer who was stalking the district undiscovered. So terrified were many of the people—non-Jews as well as Jews—that they hastily moved away. And yet Sir Robert would have us believe that there were Jews who knew the person who was committing the abominable crimes and yet carefully shielded him from the police. A more wicked assertion to put into print, without the shadow of evidence, I have seldom seen. The man whom Scotland Yard 'suspected,' subsequently, says Sir Robert, 'was caged in an asylum.' He was never brought to trial—nothing except his lunacy was proved against him. This lunatic presumably was a Jew, and because he was 'suspected,' as a result of the police 'theory' I have mentioned, Sir Robert ventures to tell the story he does, as if he were stating facts, forgetting that such a case as that of Adolph Beck was ever heard of.

But, now listen to the 'proof' Sir Robert Anderson gives of his theories. When the lunatic, who presumably was a Jew and who was suspected by Scotland Yard, was seen by a Jew—'the only person who ever had a good view of the murderer'—Sir Robert tells us he at once identified him, 'but when he learned that the suspect was a fellow-Jew he declined to swear to him.' This is Scotland Yard's idea of 'proof' positive of their 'theory'! What more natural than the man's hesitancy to identify another as 'Jack the Ripper' so soon as he knew he was a Jew? What more natural than for that fact at once to cause doubts in his mind? The crimes identified with 'Jack the Ripper' were of a nature that it would be difficult for any Jew—'low-class' or any class—to imagine the work of a Jew. Their callous brutality was foreign to Jewish nature, which, when it turns criminal, goes into quite a different channel. I confess that however sure I might have been of the identity of a person, when I was told he had been committing 'Jack the Ripper' crimes, and was a Jew, I should hesitate about the certainty of my identification, especially as anyone—outside Scotland Yard—knows how prone to mistake the clearest-headed and most careful of people are when venturing to identify anyone else. It is a matter for regret and surprise that so able a man as Sir Robert Anderson should, upon the wholly erroneous and ridiculous 'theory' that Jews would shield a raving murderer because he was a Jew, rather than yield him up to 'Gentile justice,' build up the series of statements that he has. There is no real proof that the lunatic who was 'caged' was a Jew—there is absolutely no proof that he was responsible for the 'Jack the Ripper' crimes, and hence it appears to me wholly gratuitous on the part of Sir Robert to fasten the wretched creature—whoever he was—upon our people.[7]

The London *Globe* carried an interview with Anderson, which touched upon the scathing Jewish response to his words:

When I stated that the murderer was a Jew, I was stating a simple matter of fact. It is not a matter of theory. I should be the last man in the world to say anything reflecting on the Jews as a community, but what is true of Christians is equally true of Jews—that there are some people who have lapsed from all that is good and proper. We have 'lapsed masses' among Christians. We cannot talk of 'lapsed masses' among Jews, but there are cliques of them in the East-end, and it is a notorious fact that there is a stratum of Jews who will not give up their people.

In stating what I do about the Whitechapel murders, I am not speaking as an expert in crime, but as a man who investigated the facts. Moreover, the man who identified the murderer was a Jew, but on learning that the criminal was a Jew he refused to proceed with his identification. As for the suggestion that I intended to cast any reflection on the Jews anyone who has read my books on Biblical exegesis will know the high estimate I have of Jews religiously.[8]

He then tried to appease the readers of the *Jewish Chronicle*, writing a letter that they published:

Sir,—With reference to 'Mentor's' comments on my statements about the 'Whitechapel murders' of 1888 in this month's Blackwood, will you allow me to express the sincere distress I feel that my words should be construed as 'an aspersion upon Jews.' For much that I have written in my various books gives proof of my sympathy with, and interest in, 'the people of the Covenant'; and I am happy in reckoning members of the Jewish community in London among my personal friends.

I recognise that in this matter I said either too much or too little. But the fact is that as my words were merely a repetition of what I published several years ago without exciting comment, they flowed from my pen without any consideration.

We have in London a stratum of the population uninfluenced by religious or even social restraints. And in this stratum Jews are to be found as well as Gentiles. And if I were to describe the condition of the maniac who committed these murders, and the course of loathsome immorality which reduced him to that condition, it would be manifest that in his case every question of nationality and creed is lost in a ghastly study of human nature sunk to the lowest depth of degradation.

Yours obediently,
ROBERT ANDERSON.[9]

This exchange resulted in Anderson modifying his 'Jewish comments' in the book version of the *Blackwood's* series. It is interesting to note, also, that the *Blackwood's* serialisation of *The Lighter Side of My Official Life* ended abruptly in June 1910 and was not completed.

Anderson's claims about the identity of Jack the Ripper being known was causing something of a furore with a number of newspapers picking up on the story. A solicitor called George Kebbell, rejected Anderson's claims. He believed his former client, William Grant, a sailor who had been arrested in 1895 for attacking a prostitute with a knife in the East End of London, was Jack the Ripper. She was badly wounded and Grant was sentenced to ten years for the vicious assault.[10] At his trial at the Old Bailey prosecutor Horace Avory said, 'The crime bore a strange resemblance to the Jack the Ripper murders, and the police had turned their attention to the matter without result.'[11]

Kebbell elaborated in a letter to the *Pall Mall Gazette*:

> Jack the Ripper was not a Jew but an Irishman, educated for the medical profession, and, for reasons, disowned by his relatives. This man was caught in the very act in an alley in Spitalfields. It was thoroughly recognised at the time the police had got the man at last.[12]

The publication of such controversial claims could not go unnoticed by Reid, and they didn't. The ever-vigilant Reid picked up on his old chief's claims and the others. He dismissed them all, writing from Hampton-on-Sea to the *Morning Advertiser* saying:

> What should we do if it could be proved beyond all doubt that 'Jack the Ripper' was dead? We should have to fall back upon the big gooseberry or the sea serpent for stock. Some years ago the late Major Arthur Griffiths, in his book, 'Mysteries of Crime and Police' [sic], endeavoured to prove that 'Jack's' body was found floating in the Thames seven weeks after the last Whitechapel murder on the last day of the year 1888. Considering that there were nine murders said to have been committed by 'Jack the Ripper,' I think it wonderful that the man's body should have been found in the Thames before the first of the murders were committed. I carried on a corres-pondence through the newspapers with a writer who signed himself 'Unofficial,' who tried to prove that 'Jack the Ripper,' Neill Cream, and Klosowski, alias Chapman, were all the same individual. I pointed out that both Neill Cream and Klosowski were poisoners, and that to compare their work with 'Jack the Ripper's' was like comparing the work of a watchmaker with that of a bricklayer. 'Unofficial' finished up by stating that he obtained his information from Major Griffiths' book, and expressed a wish to hear about what the Major, who was then alive, had to say about it. There was no response. Thus the matter ended. Now we have Sir Robert Anderson saying that 'Jack the Ripper' was a Jew. That I challenge him to prove; and, what is more, it was never suggested at the time of the murders. Next we have a solicitor stating that 'Jack the Ripper' was an Irishman, who had been educated for the medical profession, worked as a fireman on a cattle boat, and was arrested in the very act of mutilat-ing a woman. That is news indeed. Then we come to a statement from Dr. Forbes Winslow, who professes to know all about 'Jack the Ripper,'

and states that the last Whitechapel murder committed was that of Alice McKenzie in July 1889. The Doctor is a bit out in his statement; the last murder was Frances Coles in Swallow Gardens on 13th February 1891. Much has been said and written which is not true about certain mutilations having characterised these murders, and if Dr. Bagster Phillips, who held the post-mortems in conjunction with Dr. Percy Clark, was still alive, he would confirm my statement. Dr. Clark, who resides in Spital-square, is still alive, and knows what I say is true. The number of descriptions that have been given of 'Jack the Ripper' are truly astonishing, but I challenge anyone to prove that there was a tittle of evidence against man, woman or child in connexion with the Ripper murders. In fact, there is no proof that it was a man who committed the murders, as no man was ever seen in the company of the women who were found dead.[13]

Having been given a lead that was too good to miss, the *East London Observer* set about finding Dr Percy Clark and obtaining his opinions on the Whitechapel murders. Dr Clark had taken over the practice on the death of Dr Bagster Phillips in 1897, having previously been Phillips' assistant. To the delight of the reporter Clark 'spoke freely on the subject,' despite being of the opinion that it was probably 'better to let the matter rest.' It was the first time that Clark had, at least publicly, given his views. He pointed out the fact that the press of the day had carried all sorts of stories and that every murder that was committed was attributed to Jack the Ripper. An example was the case of the 'Pinchin Street torso', but that case, Dr Clark pointed out, 'in no way resembled those in Dorset-street and Hanbury-street.'

He continued:

All the Ripper murders were similar in character, and they were all the work of a homicidal maniac. The victims were unfortunate women of the lowest type. It is my idea that the perpetrator was a man who had become insane—probably a man of the lowest class.

One of the suppositions was that he was a medical student, or something of that sort.

There was nothing of a professional character about these wounds. The bodies were simply slashed about from head to foot.

The reporter found that Dr Clark possessed a photograph of the Dorset-street victim. 'It presents a horrible sight,' he wrote. 'The body is cut about in the most ruthless manner. Scarcely any of the face is left, and the lower limbs were lacerated.' Dr Clark went on:

Mr. Phillips did not believe in publishing details of these cases. The reporters never got the least information from him, so that a great many of the details were pure imagination.

I say he was a man not in a decent position in life, because, however low a man of that kind sinks, he would be chary of consorting with these women. If he were a sailor or a man on a cattle boat—as has been suggested—he would not be. In one case there was exhibited a certain knowledge of butchery or of killing animals, judging from the way the body was disembowelled. But there was never any justification for the suggestion that the culprit was a professional man. The Dorset-street murder was done inside a room, so that he had plenty of time. The others were committed in a court or street.

'Do you think they were all the work of one man?' the reporter asked.

'I am not so certain of that,' Dr Clark replied. 'You see, if you publish details of cases of that kind—and all the evidence at the inquests appeared in the papers—a weak-minded individual will be induced to emulate the crime, which was evidently done with a butcher's knife or a table knife. Because of this it was thought the deeds were perpetrated by a butcher or someone acquainted with the killing or cleaning of animals. It need not necessarily have been a butcher, because so many people can do that work.'

Asked if he thought one man was responsible for all the murders, Dr Clark said: 'I think perhaps one man was responsible for three of them. I would not like to say he did the others.'

'It is surely a remarkable thing that the police could get no clue,' the reporter commented.

'Not in the least,' answered Dr Clark. 'No one is more cunning than a maniac. Then, again, he would be one of the low type, of which you see thousands loafing about the streets.'

The reporter persisted. 'Isn't it rather curious that he should not have revealed himself in some way since?'

'No,' Clark replied. 'Anything may have happened to him. He may have died or got shut up in a lunatic asylum.'

'Possibly he may have no recollection of having done the deeds?'

'Possibly not.'

'Nothing like that kind of slashing as done by the murderer has ever occurred before or since?'

'No, I don't think so.'

'Mr. George R. Sims states that the man committed suicide.'

'That is really supposition,' said Clark. 'As far as I heard—and I think I heard most about the cases—there was never the slightest clue to anybody. The whole thing was theory.'

'And I suppose it will remain so?'

'It will remain so, because you could not believe the word of the man who committed these crimes even if he told you. You have only to look a that photograph to see that it is the work of a homicidal maniac.'[14]

Percy Clark would eventually leave the East End and emigrate to America.

CHAPTER NINETEEN

The City Police Suspect

> 'The mystery can never be cleared up.'
>
> Inspector Harry Cox, City Police

There has been much speculation as to the identity of the City Police suspect referred to by Swanson in his marginalia and by ex-Detective Constable Robert Sagar of the City Police. In *Reynolds News* Justin Atholl wrote that Sagar had said:

> We had good reason to suspect a man who worked in Butcher's Row, Aldgate. We watched him carefully. There was no doubt that this man was insane, and after a time his friends thought it advisable to have him removed to a private asylum. After he was removed, there were no more Ripper atrocities.[1]

The City and Metropolitan Police Forces were inextricably involved with each other in the investigation of these murders and Inspector McWilliam of the City Police liaised closely with Chief Inspector Swanson. Thus we find that Reid's counterparts in the City force also had a Jewish suspect. Most revealing of all statements by retired City officers is that of ex-Detective Inspector Harry Cox whose reminiscences were serialised in *Thomson's Weekly News*. His Ripper memoirs appeared on the front page as follows:

> Much has been written regarding the identity of the man who planned and successfully carried out the outrages. Many writers gifted with a vivid

imagination have drawn pictures for the public of the criminal whom the police suspected. All have been woefully wrong. In not a single case has one succeeded in discovering the persons [sic] who while the trail of blood lay thick and hot was looked upon as a man not unlikely to be connected with the crimes.

There are those who claim that the perpetrator was well known to the police; that at the present moment he is incarcerated in one of His Majesty's penal settlements. Others hold that he was known to have jumped over London Bridge or Blackfriars Bridge; while a third party claims that he is the inmate of a private lunatic asylum. These theories I have no hesitation in dispelling at once.

We had many people under observation while the murders were being perpetrated, but it was not until the discovery of the body of Mary Kelly had been made that we seemed to get upon the trail.

Certain investigations made by several of our cleverest detectives made it apparent to us that a man living in the East End of London was not unlikely to have been connected with the crimes.

To understand the reason we must first of all understand the motive of the Whitechapel crimes. The motive was, there can be not the slightest doubt, revenge. Not merely revenge on the few poor unfortunate victims of the knife, but revenge on womankind. It was not a lust for blood, as many people have imagined.

The murderer was a misogynist, who at some time or another had been wronged by a woman. And the fact that his victims were of the lowest class proves, I think, that he was not, as has been stated, an educated man who had suddenly gone mad. He belonged to their own class.

Had he been wronged by a woman occupying a higher stage in society the murders would in all probability have taken place in the West End, the victims have been members of the fashionable demi-monde.

The man we suspected was about five feet six inches in height, with short, black, curly hair, and he had a habit of taking late walks abroad. He occupied several shops in the East End, but from time to time he became insane, and was forced to spend a portion of his time in an asylum in Surrey.

While the Whitechapel murders were being perpetrated his place of business was in a certain street, and after the last murder I was on duty in this street for nearly three months.

There were several other officers with me, and I think there can be no harm in stating that the opinion of most of them was that the man they were watching had something to do with the crimes. You can imagine that never once did we allow him to quit our sight.

We had the use of a house opposite the shop of the man we suspected, and, disguised, of course, we frequently stopped across in the role of customers.

I shall never forget one occasion when I had to shadow our man during one of his late walks. As I watched him from the house opposite one night, it suddenly struck me that there was a wilder look than usual on his evil countenance, and I felt that something was about to happen. When darkness set in I saw him come forth from the door of his little shop and glance furtively around to see if he were being watched. I allowed him to get right out of the street before I left the house, and then I set off after him. I followed him to Lehman [sic] Street, and there I saw him enter a shop which I knew was the abode of a number of criminals well known to the police.

He did not stay long. For about a quarter of an hour I hung about keeping my eye on the door, and at last I was rewarded by seeing him emerging alone.

He made his way down to St George's in the East End, and there to my astonishment I saw him stop and speak to a drunken woman.

I crouched in a doorway and held my breath. Was he going to throw himself right into my waiting arms? He passed on after a moment or two, and on I slunk after him.

As I passed the woman she laughed and shouted something after me, which, however, I did not catch.

My man was evidently of opinion that he might be followed at every minute. Now and again he turned his head and glanced over his shoulder, and consequently I had the greatest difficulty in keeping behind him.

I had to work my way along, now with my back to the wall, now pausing and making little runs for a sheltering doorway. Not far from where the model lodging-house stands he met another woman, and for a considerable distance he walked along with her.

Just as I was beginning to prepare myself for a terrible ordeal, however, he pushed her away from him and set off at a rapid pace.

In the end he brought me, tired, weary, and nerve-strung, back to the street he had left where he disappeared into his own house.

Next morning I beheld him busy as usual. It is indeed very strange that as soon as this madman was put under observation the mysterious crimes ceased, and that very soon he removed from his usual haunts and gave up his nightly prowls. He was never arrested for the reason that not the slightest scrap of evidence could be found to connect him with the crimes.

Long after the public had ceased to talk about the murders we continued to investigate them.

We had no clue to go upon, but every point suggested by the imagination was seized upon and worked bare. There was not a criminal in London capable of committing the crimes but was looked up and shadowed.

The mystery is as much a mystery as it was fifteen years ago. It is all very well for amateur detectives to fix the crime upon this or that suspect, and advance theories in the public press to prove his guilt. They are working upon surmise, nothing more.

The mystery can never be cleared up until someone comes forward and himself proves conclusively that he was the bloodthirsty demon who terrorised the country, or unless he returns to his crimes and is caught red-handed. He is still alive then? you ask. I do not know. For all I know he may be dead. I have personally no evidence either way.[2]

Unfortunately the suspect is not positively identified, although it would appear that he was a Jew, about five feet six inches tall, with dark curly hair. He was a shop owner/keeper and was at times placed in a Surrey lunatic asylum. It highlights the fact that there certainly was no consensus of opinion amongst the police officers and adds details of yet another suspect to the long list revealed to us in the history of this unique series of Victorian murders.

CHAPTER TWENTY

Final Thoughts on the Ripper

> 'The earth has been raked over and the seas have been swept, to find this criminal 'Jack the Ripper,' always without success.'
>
> Edmund Reid

A double murder in Hanbury Street in December 1911, not far from where Annie Chapman had been murdered in 1888, raised press mention of the old Ripper murders, and probably caused Reid to resume his reminiscences. The victims were Polish Jews, Samuel and Annie Millstein, the proprietors of a thriving restaurant. About 4 a.m. on 27 December 1911, a young man living on the top floor of 62 Hanbury Street smelt smoke and heard groans that he initially ignored, 'as it seems there was an invalid woman in one of the rooms and it was thought she had been taken bad again.' The smell of smoke, however, increased and upon seeing the smoke the young man alerted the police and the fire brigade. The bodies of the Millsteins were removed from the burning ground-floor rear room, and it was discovered that they had both suffered multiple knife wounds, probably inflicted by a long knife that was found in the room. A bottle of paraffin was also found, which appeared to have been used to set fire to the mattress. The Millsteins' cash box was missing.

It was found that the Millsteins allowed their basement to be used for gambling, but the noise that this created meant that Mrs Millstein could not sleep, so Samuel had put a stop to it. The main problem had been 'a certain man [who] gets in such a way when he loses a couple of pounds', and he had been threatening Mr Millstein.[1] A twenty-eight-year-old costermonger named Meyer Abramovich confessed to the murders at Leman Street Police

Station. Coroner Baxter's inquest jury found Abramovich responsible for the murders and he was tried at the Old Bailey. He pleaded not guilty but was sentenced to death.[2] He appealed but failed; he was executed in March 1912 and was said to have died repenting of his crime.[3]

Reid was still fond of his old stamping ground and was concerned that such incidents gave Whitechapel, unfairly, a bad reputation:

> Whitechapel has an evil reputation, and one that it does not by any means deserve. During the whole time I had charge there I never saw a drunken Jew. I always found them industrious, and good fellows to live among. Even the so-called 'Whitechapel murders' were not peculiar to that division, for one was in the City of London, one in Bethnal Green, four in Spitalfields, two in St. George's, and only one in Whitechapel.

This inevitably led him to expound again upon the murders, and we can do no better than to quote his own words:

> I have been asked to tell the story of the 'Ripper' series many times, but to do so would necessitate the devotion of weeks of labour to the matter. But this I will say at once. I challenge anyone to produce a tittle of evidence of any kind against anyone. The earth has been raked over and the seas have been swept, to find this criminal 'Jack the Ripper,' always without success. It still amuses me to read the writings of such men as Dr. Anderson, Dr. Forbes Winslow, Major Arthur Griffiths, and many others, all holding different theories, but all of them wrong. I have answered many of them in print, and would only add that I was on the scene and ought to know.
>
> Here are the only known facts. The whole of the murders were done after the public houses were closed; the victims were all of the same class, the lowest of the low, and living within a quarter of a mile of each other; all were murdered within half a mile area; all were killed in the same manner. That is all we know for certain.
>
> My opinion is that the perpetrator of the crimes was a man who was in the habit of using a certain public house, and of remaining there until closing time. Leaving with the rest of the customers, with what soldiers call 'a touch of the delirium triangle,' he would leave with one of the women.
>
> My belief is that he would in some dark corner attack her with the knife and cut her up. Having satisfied his maniacal blood lust he would go away home, and the next day know nothing about it. One thing is to my mind quite certain, and that is that he lived in the district.

The police, of course, did everything possible with a view to the arrest of the man. A set of rules was laid down as to the sending for assistance immediately upon any discovery, not only to Scotland Yard, but also to everyone who was likely to be required or of assistance. And there was always a sort of interesting speculation as to who would reach the scene of a new crime first.

Inspector Abberline and Inspector Moore, with a whole staff of detective officers from other divisions and from the Yard, were sent to render every possible assistance, and there were vigilance societies formed, the members of which used to black their faces and turn their coats inside out, and adopt all sorts of fantastic disguises before they turned out. To one of the officers of this organisation the late Queen Victoria sent a letter of commendation, and the public subscribed very liberally. Officially and otherwise many thousands of pounds were spent in the effort to catch 'Jack' but he eluded us all.[4]

Reid's observations on the Whitechapel murders are at the same time valuable and flawed, as are those of so many of the police officers in their reminiscences. He was involved in the investigations into seven of the eleven murders; his first-hand experience of the events, therefore, was undeniably extensive, and his recollections of some of the incidents were very accurate.

Dr Phillips, had he been alive at the time, would not have corroborated Reid's claim that none of the victims had any body parts taken away. After the post mortem on Chapman Dr Phillips noted that 'the uterus and its appendages with the upper portion of the vagina and the posterior two-thirds of the bladder, had been entirely removed. No trace of these parts could be found.' In the case of Eddowes, both the uterus and left kidney were missing, and Kelly's heart, evidence suggested, was probably missing. However, Reid was on leave at the time of the Chapman murder, the Eddowes murder was committed in the City of London Police area, and Inspectors Abberline and Beck dealt with Kelly. Despite this, in 1888 Reid must have been aware that in three of the cases body organs were missing. No doubt his strongest memories were of those cases in which he had personal involvement with the investigation. Reid's repeated assertion that there were nine murders in the series was higher than many of his contemporaries' estimates. The Whitechapel murders series, according to the extant police files, covered, in all, eleven murders, from that of Emma Smith on 3 April 1888, to Frances Coles on 13 February 1891.

With no conviction obtained in the case it is simply not possible to state exactly which of these were perpetrated by a common offender. Using the only possible guide, that of *modus operandi*, as few as three or as many as eight could reasonably be argued. Reid probably included Smith but rejected Rose Mylett at Poplar and the Pinchin Street torso, thus leaving him with his nine.[5] Viewed in this light, the conflicting opinions of the police officers show that it all came down to personal opinion and was thus understandable that they did not all agree with each other.

From reading some of the reports in the early twentieth-century press on Reid and Jack the Ripper, it sometimes appeared that Reid had single-handedly led the hunt for the Whitechapel murderer. Reid's name and the Ripper connection were still selling newspapers, and Reid was never shy when it came to publicity. It was not his style to play down his role in the investigations, but it should also be remembered that throughout this fraught period in the history of the East End, Reid still had to take charge of the time-consuming investigation of all other serious crime in his division such as the great silk robberies shortly after the Kelly murder. Reid's questioning of the suspects Hanhart and Benelius, however, show that he was still heavily involved in the Ripper investigation. Reid's mind was set on the subject. He and his colleagues had done everything that they possibly could to track down the murderer, but they had failed. Jack the Ripper was not apprehended, and nobody knew who he was. The detective appears to have phlegmatically accepted this and while his part in the investigation would always be a part of his life, he did not allow the universal failure to find the killer affect his retirement.

CHAPTER TWENTY-ONE

A Man of Kent

'I would not be back in London for anything.'

Edmund Reid

Born in Canterbury and moving with his wife, Emily, from the seething East End back to the quiet pastures of his native Kent after retirement in the summer of 1896, Reid always liked to be known as 'a man of Kent'.[1] They took residence at Herne, a small village near the east Kent coast, not far from his native Canterbury. It could not have been more different from London as, according to one contemporary writer, Herne was a 'demure . . . ancient village. It seems a very nest—warm and snug, and green—for human life; almost consecrating it from the aching hopes and feverish expectations of the present. Who would think that the bray and roar of multitudinous London sounded but some sixty miles away.'[2]

Reid became landlord of The Lower Red Lion, a pub that had been in existence since at least 1723 which, logically enough, was adjacent to a pub called The Upper Red Lion and was noted for its tea garden. Reid had been a teetotaller until the age of thirty-six,[3] despite being raised by a mother who kept a beer house. He advertised his new premises in the *Herne Bay Press* as offering 'Best Wines and Spirits', and he welcomed all his 'old friends at his little roadside inn.'[4]

The former detective became involved in village life and in 1897 Reid sat on a committee to organise celebrations at Herne to commemorate the sixtieth year of Queen Victoria's reign.[5] The Jubilee celebrations dominated the village with garlands and streamers adorning the main street. A pageant and sports day were attended by over 400 people.[6] His pub venture, however, was short-lived. In October 1898 Reid transferred the pub's licence to James Henry Ralph.[7]

After leaving The Lower Red Lion the Reids moved just over a mile away to Mercy Villa, Stanley Road, in the coastal resort of Herne Bay. The Husband's Boats on which Reid had been employed in his youth would pass Herne Bay on their way to Margate. The town promoted itself as a health resort and boasted a remarkably low death rate. It had a population of about 7,000, which trebled during the summer months with the influx of tourists. Reid, like so many of his former Metropolitan Police colleagues, became a private investigator. Again he advertised in the *Herne Bay Press*, as a 'Pensioned Detective, Metropolitan Police, London, with 30 years experience [in fact only twenty-three years], conducts PRIVATE INQUIRIES of all descriptions with secrecy.'[8]

Reid's early retirement from the police force, and his rather brief stint as a publican, were possibly influenced by his wife's mental state. Although she had never been institutionalised before, Emily Reid was admitted on 30 April 1900 to Chartham Hospital, an East Kent lunatic asylum, from the Blean Workhouse as a pauper lunatic after an attack of mania.[9] Her medical certificate states that she was 'incoherent and wandering in speech. Picks at her bedclothes. Has a wild look in her eyes. Passed motions into bed and attempted to throw them about the place. During the night of 30th April was being violent and abusive. Screaming at top of her voice during most part of night.'[10]

She was photographed and her particulars were taken down. Emily Reid was fifty-three years old, weighed seven stone one pound (ninety-nine pounds), and her occupation was 'housewife'. She had been insane for more than two years, the cause of which was presumed to be hereditary; the form it took was mania and this was her first such attack. She was not suicidal but was considered dangerous to others. She was unclean in her habits. Her religion was Church of England, although the workhouse had recorded her as a Baptist (she had married Reid at the Baptist Chapel in Canterbury).

Emily Reid's entry in the asylum's casebook gave a brief account of her history:

Married 31 years, 2 children youngest aged 18 years. Several relatives eccentric. She herself has been affected more or less continually for some years and had headaches, sleeplessness, speech and memory both affected, was attended six months ago for paralysis. Temperate. Up to 3 weeks ago was clean and tidy at both home and herself but since then her health has been much worse. She has neglected herself.

She proved a difficult patient and her mental and physical condition deteriorated rapidly. She was attended by William Everett, who made regular notes on her condition:

On admission—She is thin and poorly nourished also very feeble and can hardly walk. She has brown hair. Eyes blue pupils equal. Will not protrude her tongue. Pulse 120 weak. Muscles easily compressible. She's very restless. Becomes excited, querulous and emotional. Resists and fights when being examined and repeats out loud again a series of oaths. Does not give a sensible answer.

3rd May—Is very restless and destructive. In padded room. Takes nourishment well. Not rational in any way.

7th May—She is suffering from mania her condition is acute. She is senseless and confused. Talks incoherently. She is in poor health. The marks on the body on admission were bruise on left eye and thigh and right knee. Old scars on legs and left thigh.

14th May—Has been quieter then restless but is now confused rambling noisy and restless. Very thin. Takes food well. Does not dress herself.

21st May—Is very noisy and excited. Constantly talking incoherently. Emotional then controlled. Takes food well. Clean in habits.

28th May—She is noisy sleepless at night. Excited and very restless. She takes food well.

29th June—She's very restless excited and noisy. Destructive and takes off her clothes. Not clean in her habits. Takes food well. Thin. Sleepless.

29th July—Has been quieter but is troublesome again. Does not dress herself. Is not clean. Restless excitable. Has nurse give her food. Noisy at night. Thin.

12th August—Very excited and restless and has been in padded room in bed for some days. Takes liquid nourishment fairly well when it's given. Has become much feebler. No rise in temperature.[11]

Emily Jane Reid died at 8.10 a.m. on 14 August 1900, of chronic organic brain disease.[12]

The information that Emily Reid was from an eccentric family and thus inherently insane was probably based on the fact that another member of her family had been mentally ill, rather than any hard evidence that the illness was known to be inherited. Emily was the daughter of an illiterate labourer, John Wilson, and Ann Cooper from Canterbury. She had five sisters and three brothers. Her younger brother, John, was recorded as an idiot in the 1871 census.

The 1901 census records that two visitors were staying with Reid at Mercy Villa. Mary Puta, a 54 year old German widow and four-year-old Mary Fewerstien from Aldgate, East London.[13] When the census enumerator visited Reid again a decade later his visitors were still with him but now they were his housekeeper and domestic servant. By then Reid had moved to nearby Hampton-on-Sea, a tiny hamlet of Herne Bay. Hampton had achieved some notoriety in earlier centuries as a location favoured by smugglers. It had a pub called the Hampton Inn and a pier built by the Oyster Fishing Company. Reid bought No. 4, Eddington Gardens,[14] and named it 'Reid's Ranch'. Two years before Reid moved into the 'Ranch' it had been advertised along with No. 3 Eddington Gardens, as:

> Two superior built seven-roomed houses, having a frontage of 19 feet with verandas, from which there is a beautiful Sea View, situated in a healthy position. Good Investment. No. 4 with Four Plots of Land adjoining, Lodge, &c., on same, £300.[15]

Reid's Ranch became nearly as well known as its owner, whose slightly eccentric nature was reflected in the building's appearance and contents. Most noticeably, the end wall of the 'Ranch' was painted with battlements and protruding cannons. Another Hampton resident, Frank Mount, recalled them in his reminiscences of Hampton. Mount commented on Reid's foresight in placing guns on the gable 'to let rip at the Germans when they come.'[16]

Soon after Reid moved in with a pet parrot for company, he received a visit from a local reporter who was keen to interview Hampton's resident celebrity, 'who knew something of the criminal life of great London.' The reporter was 'not in the least degree disappointed' in meeting Reid, 'a man whose personality was associated with some of the greatest atrocities of these latter days.' Reid and his parrot were waiting in the garden, and the journalist was quickly put at ease by 'something in the ex-detective's face.' They shook hands, 'and I took the proffered hand without feeling in the least respect inclined to seize my cap and make tracks.'

Lighting a cigar Reid had given him, the reporter 'WWS' sat back in a chair 'for the next 10 minutes,' whilst 'Reid was pouring some real detective stories into my ears.' 'WWS' went on to describe the 'Ranch'. It was:

> within a couple of hundred yards or so to the sea, and is a well arranged cottage, to which is attached an excellent lawn, a vegetable garden, a wooden structure at which thirsty pedestrians may be supplied with minerals. In the distance is a piece of water immortalised by 'mine host' as the 'Lavender Brook' [the stagnant Hampton Brook], where Reid, with just the suspicion of a merry twinkle in his eyes, told me he intended to suggest trout fishing should be introduced.

The walls of 'Reid's Ranch' were 'liberally dressed' with framed London newspapers detailing his involvement with the Whitechapel murders. On the mantelpiece stood a photograph of John Canham Read, the Southend murderer. There was also a photograph of Reid wearing Canham Read's scarf pin. The case of John Canham Read had caused a sensation in 1894. Canham Read, a middle-aged philanderer, had lived in Stepney with his wife and eight children and worked as a clerk at the nearby Royal Albert Docks.

John Canham Read had murdered his pregnant lover, 23-year-old Florence Dennis, at Southend when his amazingly tangled love life had become too much for him. Her married sister, Mrs Ayriss, with whom he had been having an affair since 1882, had introduced Canham Read to Florence in 1892. He was simultaneously seeing a Miss Kempton, with whom he had a child. Working with the Essex Constabulary, Inspector Reid kept Canham Read's Stepney house under observation and questioned the fugitive murderer's wife and friends.[17] Canham Read was eventually arrested at Mitcham, Surrey. He was tried, found guilty at Chelmsford Assizes and executed in December 1894.[18] His brother, Harry, who had reluctantly given evidence against him, committed suicide in Regent's Canal six months later.[19]

Crime writer H.L. Adam discussed the case with Reid some years later:

> I agreed with Inspector Reid that both the Reads were most interesting men to talk to. They were well educated and refined.
>
> 'Canham Read was bad at heart, and stood at nothing to satisfy his lust,' was the comment of my friend, ex-Chief [sic] Inspector Reid.[20]

'WWS' was distracted while leafing through some of Charles Gibbon's novels that Reid possessed, when 'music stole into the air. Reid was favouring me with a popular selection on some bells. By that I discovered he knew something about music.' Reid escorted the reporter onto the lawn of the 'Ranch' and regaled him with more stories for another twenty minutes, before 'human forms on the slopes hard by Hampton Inn warned Reid that he had a task to perform, and with a cheery shake of the hand the ex-detective bid me adieu, instructing me to wend my way back to the "Lavender Brook" via "Reid's Bridge." I did so.'[21]

The 'wooden structure' mentioned by the reporter was, in fact, a shed at the bottom of the garden. Reid had named it the 'Hampton-on-Sea Hotel', and from there he sold lemonade and postcards—scenes of 'Disappearing Hampton-on-Sea' and the damage caused by coastal erosion, plus several views of the 'Ranch', most featuring the by-now white-bearded and portly figure of Edmund Reid. He posted a notice advertising his 'Hotel' that read:

> It is simply wonderful that you can obtain for the price of one Penny photographic postcards at the Fine art Gallery under the flag shewing a Storm, and the 12 Houses that have been washed away during the past 18 months out of the 17 which formerly constituted the whole of Hampton-on-Sea, Kent.
>
> Please apply at the Hampton-on-Sea Grand Hotel, now being used as a mineral water Bar by direction of Mr. Lloyd George. God save the King.

The 'Lavender Brook' and 'Reid's Bridge' would come to the fore in the future. Proximity to the sea meant that Reid had to live with the threat of coastal erosion, and the 'Ranch' would eventually fall victim to the sea after his departure.

CHAPTER TWENTY-TWO

Kentish Adventures

> 'His frequent amusing letters to the Press will be recalled.'
>
> *Herne Bay Press*

Reid's long-standing relationship with the press continued unabated through his final years. He was an avid reader of the newspapers and frequently wrote to them with his views and ideas on many subjects. They were often critical of local government and officialdom. Indeed, his first letters to the *Herne Bay Press* were dispatched soon after his arrival at Herne and concerned drainage at Lower Herne.

A local Councillor, Mr Gates, had alleged that 'a nuisance is caused at Lower Herne by persons pumping the contents of their cesspools into the road, not only at one place but at every place.' Reid immediately responded in anger: 'Now this statement is not true, and I challenge him to prove it. It is a great pity that men when appointed to an office do not confine themselves to the truth.'[1] Gates defended himself then accused Reid of 'acting as the official mouthpiece' of other Herne residents although he had lived there for less than a year and had probably never heard of Lower Herne, which in fact was very close to where Reid lived.[2]

Reid could not let this stand and a week later his reply appeared accusing Councillor Gates of 'extreme ignorance' adding 'Why if it is such a dirty place, I ought to smell it, which I have not done yet. Again what a bad opinion he must have of the good people of Lower Herne to think that they cannot speak for themselves, and require a mouthpiece.'[3] Stung by the criticism Gates asked 'why has Mr Reid singled me out for attack, when other members of the Council have made statements quite as strong as I did.' The newspaper's editor called an end to the dispute saying that it 'must now cease.'[4]

Two years later Reid presented his dream of the future of Herne suggesting that living conditions there were still quite primitive. 'Does not a vision of glory float before our very eyes? Only to think of being able to think of being able to retire to rest at night without the thought of the water stealing into our homes like a thief to damp our spirits and destroy our health. Then again fancy being able to cross any road without finding yourself stuck fast (perhaps never to move again) in mud, the accumulation of years.'[5]

Reid's misfortunes in attempting to take a day trip to Canterbury in August 1899 resulted in an amusing letter to the press, pleading for a direct train service to be provided between Herne Bay and Canterbury. It had all begun when Reid enquired of a local man how best he should get there:

'What shall I do?'

'You ask for the 'Old Toll House' in Canterbury Road and wait till the Motor Car come along at 2.'

Well, I go to the Canterbury Road and when I get there, the Toll House was not there, it was pulled down. Well, I wait, and the Motor Car was come along and I was get in the road and cry out 'stop!' and the car was stop, I say to the driver, 'I want to go to a place called Canterbury,' and he say, 'you stop here and I come back for you,' it was then 20 to 2, and I go to 'Scott's' and buy a newspaper, and sit down on the roadside to read and wait for the Motor Car, but no Motor was come. I get up and say to an other man, 'When is the Motor Car coming,' and he say 'Go into Mount's fruit shop and see the card.' Well, I go into Mount's fruit shop and me make a purchase, and see the card at the back of the shop, and it say, 'Motor Car leave Herne Bay, 5 p.m.' Well, I come outside and say to a man 'I want to go to Canterbury,' and he say 'Stop here and the pair horse brake was come along and you go.' Well, I was wait and wait when a brake was come along, not four horses, and it say 'To Sturry.' I say 'Stop' and the man behind he call out 'You stop, full up.' Well, I was walk along to a place called 'Herne,' and sit down and read mine paper, and no four horses was come along, and I say to a man with fish, 'When do I get to Canterbury,' and he say, 'I do not know,' and I was ask a sergeant who was on a bicycle and he say, 'walk along till you get to the 'Red Lion' and stop till the 'Tally Ho' bus was come along and get on that.' Well, I was walk along till I get to the 'Red Lion,' when I go inside and say to a big fat man, 'When I get to Canterbury,' and he say, 'stop.' Well it was all stop, and I did stop and have a nice good tea, and then the big fat man behind the bar say, 'come on Sir,' and I was run out and the man on the bus was say, 'full up,' so I was again stop, then I say to the big fat man, 'what I do now' and he say, 'take the bus from the Church to Eddington Lane, and walk to the station and catch the train that calls at Herne Bay at 6.51 for Whitstable.' Well, I was take the bus that left the Church at 6.30 and was ride to Eddington Lane and get out and walk to the Station, and when I walk by the Hop Gardens I was see a train go and stop at the Station and go away before I was get there, I was call out, 'I want to go to Whitstable,' but they was not hear me, and I again stop and while I was outside the Railway Station I was see my bus come from the Church, and I say to the driver, 'I was not catch the train to Whitstable for Canterbury,' and he say, 'the Motor Car just gone to Canterbury.' Well, I wait and say the car was started one hour and three-quarters later than advertised, and I then take a train, 7.25, and get to Whitstable, 7.45. I say to the man on the platform, 'I want to go to Canterbury,' and he say, 'you must go to the South-Eastern Railway Station and stop till 9.' Well, I make my way to the station and stop, and when the train was come in I was get into a nice carriage where it say 'to seat five persons,' and when I was sit down there were 17 childs come in and it was very lively. I was listen to their voices singing 'We wont go home till morning.' Well, Mr. Editor, I got to Canterbury at 9.30 having started at 20 to 2, and the distanced I was go I have been told was about 9 miles, and if you was think that that was too long will you try and get a train to take the visitors much quicker, then you will have the thanks of the visitors to Herne Bay who cannot always trust the Omnibus, Motor Car, and the brakes . . . I hope, Mr. Editor, you will forgive me for troubling you, but I did try to get back to Canterbury quick and wanted to get back to my family same night at Herne Bay, but could not. What with waiting, walking, the dust and the 17 childs I was nearly deaded.[6]

The following month Reid again had cause for complaint. On this occasion a trip to London left him asking the question, 'What constitutes luggage?' Reid made a weekly trip to London, carrying a small bag. One Sunday at Holborn Station one of the staff cautioned him, 'you cannot have that bag with you in the train.' Reid asked why not and was told, 'I not pass it.' He was then delayed while his bag was weighed, during which time his train departed. Shortly afterwards Reid returned to London and visited the fish market, where he purchased some fish that was packed in a box. He went to the parcel office at Cannon Street and said, 'I want to send this parcel to Herne Bay, will it be delivered today?' He was promised that it would be, at the price of seven pence. The parcel was not delivered until three o'clock the following day, when Reid was told he would have to pay another shilling. He refused, saying, 'You will take that stinking fish away before it kills me.' His letter to the press about this incident ends as follows: 'I think that small parcels that one carries in the hand and not handed to porters to label or carry should be allowed without so much fuss and inconvenience caused by those who promise to give us so much when they [sic] two lines were made into one.'[7]

Problems with the rail service were a recurrent theme for Reid, and in 1900 he was again writing to the press about it. His grievance on this occasion was the lack of trains to Whitstable from Canterbury. He recounted an incident when he took the 7.10 p.m. train from Canterbury to Whitstable (the last train available) and was obliged to spend two hours waiting for the 9.39 train to Herne Bay at the Salvation Army Barracks and later at a pub, together with several others, 'drinking, smoking, telling tales, and grumbling because they could not get home to their wives and families till past 10.' Reid felt that there should be a nine o'clock train from Canterbury to Whitstable to avoid unnecessary delays. 'This would not be asking much, it is bad enough for men to have to wait about but what about the women who have no where to go to, not even a decent waiting-room.'[8]

While Reid was working as a private detective he gave his opinion on the lack of sufficient police strength at Herne Bay: 'There is no doubt that the present number who do the best they can under the circumstances are over-worked, and that every summons granted, and prisoner arrested, neces-sitates their attendance at Canterbury to give their evidence, and so draw them from duty here and leave the Bay and neighbourhood unprotected on the very day that their services are required most, that of Saturday.' He advocated a Petty Sessional (magistrates') Court at Herne Bay and admitted that 'I have myself advised some of my friends not to charge persons who have committed some small offences because of the loss of time and out-of pocket expenses which would be incurred if they did so, and thus the persons have escaped that punishment which could have been meted out to them had we had a little Court here that I hope to see before long.'[9]

A 1900 exchange saw Reid responding to the proposal of an earlier correspondent who called himself 'Spes' and proposed that all visitors to Herne Bay should be taxed a shilling a head. Reid agreed and, with his tongue placed firmly in cheek, suggested the building of 'a stout wall from the East to the West of Herne Bay, with a moat outside, and facing each road let there be drawbridges and turnstiles in charge of good men and true, while the wall shall be patrolled both night and day by our Volunteers, those on night duty to be supplied with search lights to prevent tunnelling, or any evil disposed person from endeavouring to enter by means of a flying machine, or balloon.' He added: 'Let our Council buy up a few ironclads which shall be anchored off the Bay well supplied with tried men and quick-firing guns to prevent anyone landing on our beautiful shore without paying the shilling.'[10]

Reid was a member of the Herne Bay Literary Society, which in 1901 heard a paper on the subject, 'Is a woman the lesser man?' Reid thought that this was the case:

and in many instances the much lesser. I shall never forget . . . the many mistakes that have happened in this world of ours by women trying to take the place of men in public matters, when their time could have been better employed with domestic duties.

I know of my own personal knowledge of women over 20 years of age who can read, write, sing and play, but not have the remotest idea of how to perform a single household duty. What a bright prospect for a man who does not look behind the scene in time. And while this state of affairs goes on in England 'women must be the lesser man,' till the sun stands still.[11]

In 1909 a letter regarding stumps of piles in the water at Hampton-on-Sea in the *Herne Bay Press* caused Reid to take up his pen again. He hoped that the Council:

will take no steps to warn the world at large of their existence because they are our only protection against a raid of some bloodthirsty pirates on our fishing fleet, which now consists of three boats, or, worse still, the invasion of some German dreadnoughts to our beautiful shore.

Until recently we were in dread that some attempt might be made to enter the lavender brook, and if my information is correct an attempt was made some little time ago, but owing to the smell of the double distilled lavender it was found too much for the raiders and they beat a hasty retreat . . .

What a glorious thing it would be to wake up some morning and see some German dreadnoughts resting on the tops of the stumps like weathercocks, while our Territorials (of which we boast two members) are peppering away at them for all they are worth.'[12]

Reid's habit of flying the Union Jack from a flagpole in the back garden of the 'Ranch' was queried in an editorial in the *Herne Bay Press*.[13] Reid replied thusly: 'I shall be pleased to confide a great secret to any of your dear readers that care to pay me a visit next Sunday, when the same flag will be flying.'[14]

A letter in the press in 1912 from the Rev. W Springthorpe objecting to the granting of occasional licences for Herne Bay's Grand Pier Pavilion brought the comment from Reid that churches are 'being sold by auction, and chapels being turned into picture shows all over London, because people will not be led by the nose as in olden times.'[15]

In 1912 a water main being laid at Hampton-on-Sea attracted Reid's interest. A cannon ball was found three feet beneath the ground that Reid claimed as his own. Coincidentally another cannon ball had been presented to Herne Bay, and a correspondent wrote to the *Herne Bay Press* in the hope that Reid would donate his cannon ball as a gift also. Reid declined on the grounds that Herne Bay had no museum and he wanted to add it to his own collection, which already boasted the post that had stood at the end of Hampton pier. This now stood on his lawn, looking 'like a 'Cleopatra Needle,' with initials on it—no doubt by boys who are now granddads.'[16]

Reid's final letter to the *Herne Bay Press* was published on Christmas Day 1915. In it he lamented the folly of war but acknowledged its necessity. 'This must be a fight to the finish, or what would our wounded say; what would the fathers and mothers say; what would the rest of the world say if England were to cry, 'Hold, enough,' after sending our sons to fight and die for Old England, the land of the free?' His own son, Harold, was fighting in France, and Reid added: 'Should he fall I shall not complain, because I shall then know that he gave his life for his friends. God save the King!'[17]

CHAPTER TWENTY-THREE

Building Bridges

> 'A gentleman living in Hampton who has obliterate the word 'impossible' from his dictionary.'
>
> *Herne Bay Press*

If Edmund Reid thought that on retiring he had attended his last coroner's inquest he was wrong. On Monday 11 August 1902, labourer William Lingham found the body of a man who had been washed ashore at the foot of the cliff on the west side of Hampton Pier. Lingham thought that the deceased had the appearance of a bargeman. PC Butcher of Herne Bay saw the body transported to an outbuilding of the Hampton Inn. Butcher judged the body to have been in the water for at least a month and guessed the age at about thirty-five years, adding: 'His length was 5ft. 11in., and he was a stoutly built man. Deceased had very dark hair, rather inclined to be wavy, and heavy dark eyebrows. He also had the appearance of a mariner.' The body was dressed in two pairs of trousers, blue serge on the outside and a pair of light striped tweeds underneath, and wore a blue striped flannelette shirt, two pairs of brown socks, and a pair of deck boots. Butcher searched the body and found two shilling pieces, a piece of brass, a piece of string, and a box of what he thought might be Swedish matches.

Reid had witnessed the removal of the body to the inn and was chosen as foreman of the jury at the inquest held two days later at the Hampton Inn. He told the inquest that the deceased's description had been circulated but no one had been found who could identify him. He added: 'The body was not overhauled in any way before its removal to the inn.' The jury returned a verdict of 'found dead'. Before the inquest closed Reid thought he should let the coroner know that the removal of the body from the sea was carried out in a 'discreet and decent way by the constable.' In Reid's opinion, 'It was very satisfactory to be able to bear such testimony, having regard to the time of year and the large number of visitors passing to and fro in that locality.'[1]

Almost nine years later to the day Reid was again present at a coroner's inquest for a drowning at Hampton, but this time as a witness. At about 11 a.m. on Thursday 10 August 1911 he saw unemployed riveter John Smith, sixty-two years old, accost two men in Hampton and ask them for sixpence. The men refused and Smith then went through Herne Cliff Garden towards Whitstable, before going down to the ruined concrete wall near the site of some cottages that had been removed due to coastal erosion.

Smith began undressing and a surprised Reid told him: 'Clear out.' 'I am going to have a swim,' Smith replied. 'You are not going to bathe here,' Reid said; 'you have no bathing dress,' to which Smith retorted, 'I don't care, I am going to swim; I have not had one for two years.' Smith then went around the ruins of the sea walls into the sea. Reid watched him swim out and then float a few yards into the sea. Reid left but returned five minutes later and saw that Smith was evidently in difficulty some distance away. He thought about attempting to rescue Smith but there was a drop of ten feet to the ruined wall, and even if he could have made it to the water Reid did not consider himself a good enough swimmer to be able to help him. Instead he went for assistance but could find no one; upon returning he saw Smith turn over onto his face and float farther away before disappearing. Smith's body was eventually recovered at about 6.20 p.m. on the shore halfway between Herne Bay Pier and Hampton Pier.

The inquest was held the following day at the town hall, where it was revealed that Smith (who also used the name Sullivan 'when he got into trouble') was of no fixed abode and had not been in regular work for many years. A plasterer, Stanley Panton, who had been with him earlier that day, had identified him. Smith had appeared to be sober and in his usual health. Reid gave his evidence and a juror supported his claim that he could not have climbed down the cliff, saying, 'It would be a difficult feat for an active man to get down there at this point, as the cliff was perfectly straight, and Mr. Reid could not have managed it.' The cause of death, according to the doctor, was drowning, possibly brought about by an attack of cramp. A verdict of 'death by misadventure' was returned.[2]

Reid probably read the account in the *Herne Bay Press* of another local inquest, that of Bessie Williams (nee Munday) that took place in Herne Bay in July 1912.[3] Death by misadventure was the jury's verdict on the unfortunate woman who had drowned in her bath. The newspaper noted that upon hearing the verdict her, 'husband was again very greatly distressed.' George Joseph Smith was the husband and one of the most notorious murderers of the twentieth century. Smith bigamously married a number of women, fleeced them of their money before deserting, or in three instances, murdering his brides by drowning them in baths.

George Smith was eventually arrested in 1915. The body of Bessie Williams was exhumed from Herne Bay Cemetery and Smith was tried and sentenced to death. The 'Brides in the Bath' murderer was so loathed that even hangman John Ellis commented, 'I was really glad I was given the opportunity to hang this man.'[4] Had Edmund Reid, celebrated detective of the nineteenth century, passed Smith, reviled murderer of the twentieth century, on the Herne Bay seafront, blithely unaware of his crimes?

The proximity of 'Reid's Ranch' to the sea exposed Reid to the problems of coastal erosion, decomposing seaweed (which gave birth to the 'Lavender Brook'), and silt deposition, which caused low-lying land to become flooded. This was to result in a battle between the remaining residents of Hampton and the local Council, a dispute that was to run for many years.

In 1909 Reid complained that Hampton-on-Sea had 'no roads, paths, lights, sewer, water, or dust collector, nor any residents receiving parish relief despite an annual payment of £40 in rates.' He was also concerned that the footbridge connecting Hampton to Herne Bay was in an 'unsafe condition. Some of the boards were loose, some broken, which have not been attended to, so that the bridge is still out of repair and dangerous to the public at large.' The parish council inspected the footbridge and reported that 'it appeared to be quite safe. To satisfy the residents of Hampton, however, the surveyor should certainly make an examination.'[5]

Writing to the press Reid attacked the council's lack of bridge maintenance: 'Of course, I quite understand the enormous expense it would be to re-paint it, quite 10s.' The council reiterated that they 'had visited it and found it alright.' According to Reid, 'hundreds of people who have passed over it' could prove that the footbridge was not all right. He had 'pointed out that what was wanted were two iron bands to run along the sides to keep the boards from being raised by the high tides—not a few nails.' He regretted that no one from the council had visited him in person, 'as I only reside a few yards from the bridge in question, because it would be better than trying to show that my complaints are groundless.'[6]

Reid decided to take matters into his own hands, and 'at a point near the old culvert caused a bridge to be erected. It has already proved of convenience to those desiring to reach the cottages at Hampton.' He, along with two others, had built the bridge in three days at a cost of £3. He sent a bill for £3 to the council, along with a photograph of himself standing on the new bridge. An accompanying letter pointed out that the building of the bridge 'was entirely in consequence of their neglect to provide a means of access to the houses in this part of their district.' Reid revealed that he had received 20s. 6d., plus several promises towards his expenses from fellow Hampton residents; 'so as you can see,' he remarked, 'bridge building is not a paying concern.'[7] The council returned Reid's bill but now acknowledged that the old bridge was unsafe, and they placed a notice by it warning the public. The sign was deemed 'laughable' by Reid. 'If dangerous, repair it. What I would respectfully beg to suggest is that the word 'useless' be put up instead.'[8]

The notice board lasted for only five days before it went missing. It was the opinion of the council's surveyor that 'it was evident that someone had wrenched it from the post.' Reid innocently suggested that 'in fact Halley's Comet came along on the 8th, and was so disgusted that he knocked the board off with his tail.' As far as the old bridge was concerned, 'the danger is past. The bridge rests on beach; not a drop of water underneath.' Still he pleaded with the council to 'do their duty and clear the brook of the thousands of tons of beach they have allowed to block the mouth, and thus prevent the storm water from going through its proper course.'[9] The dispute would continue for years to come, but Reid left it for others, as he had become involved in an entirely different argument.

CHAPTER TWENTY-FOUR

Desecrating the Sabbath

'His death was rather sudden.'

Herne Bay Press

The former editor of the *Herne Bay Press*, prominent Herne Bay resident James Watkinson, took umbrage at the close of the 1910 holiday season to the local council's allowing public entertainment to be held on the pier on Sundays. He felt that 'most right thinking people have deplored the desecration of the Sabbath.'[1]

Edmund Reid, together with 1,500 others, had attended the last Sunday band concert; they had 'received their money's worth and came away happy. Where,' he wondered, 'is the preacher who could bring 1,500 people to pay 4*d*. with pleasure, entertain them for two hours, and send them away feeling that the time had not been misspent in listening to sweet music, and singing such as gladdens the heart of man, woman, and child.'

Reid 'could not help thinking what would a vicar of a church, or a pastor of a chapel, give to have such a congregation before them. If our churches and chapels are empty, what is the cause? People now think for themselves, expand their minds and see that the church has lost its power over the people.' He declared himself to be a 'free agent' who would 'rest in peace until next season, with the assurance that the band will play and the singers sing to the enjoyment of 1,500 people.'

Reid's letter received support from fellow 'free agents' who thought that Watkinson 'manifested an extreme and uncharitable spirit towards those who prefer to spend their Sunday in a manner that appeals to their conscience. We do not find as a rule these people doing all in their power to prevent Mr Watkinson from spending Sunday as his inclinations direct.' Reid also felt that Watkinson was imposing his beliefs unnecessarily, saying that 'I am not a teetotaller, but a long way from it; yet I don't suppose I enter a public-house once a month, yet do not go without a good drop of Scotch, which I pour down my own throat and anybody's that like it. I consider this better than blowing tobacco smoke into other people's faces if they like it or not.'[2]

Ignoring his other critics, Watkinson focused on Reid,[3] who responded two days later by pointing out 'that the Sabbath was not desecrated, the entertainment was good, and the time and money was well spent.' By now this public argument was becoming quite heated, and many readers of the *Herne Bay Press* were taking sides and writing letters. Perhaps in a conciliatory tone Reid let it be known that 'I have every respect for anyone who holds different opinions to myself as long as they fight fair and keep to the point, no matter what may be our calling in life,' adding that if he had known 'others more able to answer Mr. James Watkinson's letter intended to do so, I should not have done it.'[4]

Watkinson replied in a very non-confrontational manner and finished by saying that 'with this letter I drop my correspondence with Mr. Reid, as I have no desire to waste my time or your space further in dealing with the question from the purely personal standpoints.' Reid also dropped the correspondence and the matter came to a close.[5] In 1912 Mr Watkinson was elected President of the Herne Bay Historical Society. Reid wrote again to the Press, expressing his pleasure at the appointment of 'our old friend. It will be in good hands and may it flourish.'[6]

In 1916 Reid left the 'Ranch' and returned to Herne Bay, moving into 6 Pier Avenue, known as 'Palm Villa'. The move was probably a result of the rapidly encroaching sea that had already claimed twelve other properties in Hampton in 1911, an event commemorated by a signpost Reid erected on the site of the houses.[7] Coastal erosion was such a serious problem, particularly at low lying Hampton whose archaic coastal defences were no match for the encroaching sea that had swallowed up houses, gardens and a croquet lawn. The issue was featured in a London newspaper. Under the headline 'Herne Bay Becoming a Peninsula' in the *Morning Leader*, a photograph showed Reid inspecting a partially demolished property.[8]

Reid did not witness the resolution of the 1914-18 conflict. In May 1917 he remarried. His new wife was Lydia Rhoda Halling, the spinster daughter of an army officer. She was over twenty years Reid's junior.

On Monday 3 December 1917 Reid, 'apparently in the best of health arranged to attend an entertainment in the evening.' Shortly before he was due to go out, 'he was taken seriously ill.' Dr T.A. Bowes was called but nothing could be done to help Reid, who died at 6.45 a.m. on Wednesday 5 December 1917,[9] of chronic interstitial nephritis and cerebral haemorrhage.

His local newspaper, the *Herne Bay Press*, in whose pages Reid's name had so often featured, printed an affectionate obituary. Edmund Reid, they fondly recalled, had been 'a man of kindly heart. A man of much geniality he was a good companion, and he could keep one interested for hours by reminiscences drawn from his long and varied experience, many of them of an exciting character. He was a man of whimsical humour . . . he could put some telling points into a letter, and he would persist in his agitation till it was successful.'[10]

Edmund Reid's funeral took place at Herne Bay Cemetery on the afternoon of 8 December. His widow as well as his daughter Elizabeth, and his son Harold, now a sergeant in the army, attended, together with his sister-in-law, Hetty Halling.[11] Reid's widow, Lydia, having been married for barely more than six months, never remarried and died twenty-one years later at St. Leonard's-on-Sea near Hastings, where she lived with her spinster sister Eunice. She was remembered by her friends as 'a sweet little lady.'[12]

Thus ended the eventful life of the man who could truly claim, amongst his other adventures, to have hunted Jack the Ripper. Reid's prediction that future generations of his family would follow in his footsteps did not prove correct. None did.[13]

Notes

PRO – *Public Record Office documents held at the National Archives*

CHAPTER ONE – THE MAKING OF A POLICE OFFICER

1   *Lloyd's Weekly News*, 4 February 1912.
2   Ibid.
3   PRO MEPO 4/352.
4   *Lloyd's Weekly News*, 4 February 1912.
5   PRO MEPO 7/36.
6   *Lloyd's Weekly News*, 4 February 1912.
7   PRO MEPO 7/40.
8   *Times*, 10 October 1888.
9   *Police Review and Parade Gossip*, 12 June 1896.
10 *Chelmsford Chronicle*, 19 October 1877.
11 PRO MEPO 7/42.
12 PRO MEPO 7/45.
13 *Lloyd's Weekly News*, 4 February 1912.
14 Charles Gibbon, By *Mead and Stream*, Vol 3, London, Chatto and Windus, 1884.
15 *Yarmouth Mercury*, 23 August 1890.
16 *Herne Bay Press*, 27 September 1902.
17 *Weekly Dispatch*, 8 March 1896.
18 *Police Review and Parade Gossip*, 12 June 1896. Queen of the Meadow was also the name of a novel published in 1880 by Reid's friend Charles Gibbon.
19 *Lloyd's Weekly News*, 4 February 1912.

Chapter Two – East End Detective

1   PRO MEPO 7/48.
2   *Weekly Dispatch*, 8 March 1896.
3   PRO CRIM 10/76. *Times*, 23, 30 August, 15, 20, September 1886.
4   *Weekly Dispatch*, 8 March 1896.
5   *Toby*, 5 March 1887.
6   *Toby*, 21 May 1887.
7   PRO MEPO 7/49.
8   *Toby*, 21 September 1889.
9   *East London Observer*, 17 December 1887.
10 PRO MEPO 7/49.

Chapter Three – 1888

Unless otherwise stated all information concerning the Whitechapel Murders in subsequent chapters is taken from Stewart P Evans and Keith Skinner, The Ultimate Jack the Ripper Sourcebook, London, Constable & Robinson, 2000 and Philip Sugden, The Complete History of Jack the Ripper, New York, Carroll & Graf, 2002.

1   Metropolitan Police Commissioner's Annual Report, 1888, in private hands.
2   W.J. Gordon, *How London Lives*, London, Religious Tract Society, 1890.
3   In the first edition of this book the authors suggested the possible origin of the name could have been with one 'Tot Fay', an habitual female drunkard of the period who appeared in *Reynolds's Newspaper* and who was suggested in *The Jack the Ripper A-Z* (1996) as 'Tottie Fay.' In 2000 author Melvin Harris sent the song sheet of 'Polly Wolly Doodle' to Stewart Evans suggesting that as the actual source. The authors also note with interest that 'Fairy Fay' was the name of a well-known racing dog of the 1890s.
4   *Reynolds News*, 29 October 1950.
5   *Lloyd's Weekly Newspaper*, 8 April 1888.
6   London Metropolitan Archives St. B.G./Wh/123/19.

Chapter Four – Murder in George Yard

1   PRO HO 65/62.
2   *East London Observer*, 11 August 1888.
3   *East London Observer*, 25 August 1888.
4   *East London Advertiser*, 25 August 1888.
5   *Lloyd's Weekly Newspaper*, 26 August 1888.

Chapter Five – The Whitechapel Murders

1   Robert Anderson, *The Lighter Side of My Official Life*, London, Hodder & Stoughton, 1910.
2   Her name was sometimes spelt 'Darrell' in the newspapers.

Chapter Six – Hunting the Maniac

1   Metropolitan Police Commissioner's Report of 15 September 1888, in private hands.
2   Shane Leslie, *Sir Evelyn Ruggles-Brise*, London, John Murray, 1938.
3   Robert Anderson, *The Lighter Side of My Official Life*, London, Hodder & Stoughton, 1910.

Chapter Seven – Suspects

1   *Star*, 5 September 1888.

Chapter Eight – Double Atrocity

1   *Star*, 1 October 1888.
2   *Star*, 2 October 1888.
3   *Times*, 6 October 1888.
4   *Evening News* (Portsmouth), 2 October 1888.
5   All inquest reports taken from *Daily Telegraph*, *East London Advertiser*, *East London Observer*, *Lloyd's Weekly Newspaper* and the *Times*.
6   *Reynolds's Newspaper*, 7 April 1895.
7   *Star of the East*, 1 October 1888.

CHAPTER NINE – JACK THE RIPPER

1 Both Anderson and Macnaghten believed the letter and postcard to be the work of a journalist and in 1913 ex-Chief Inspector Littlechild named Thomas Bulling of the Central News Agency as the journalist believed by Scotland Yard to be responsible. Warren also thought the letter to be a hoax.

2 *Morning Advertiser*, 4 October 1888.

3 PRO HO 65/62.

4 *Morning Advertiser*, 4 October 1888.

5 *Sunday Times*, 21 October 1888.

6 Leonard Archer, private letter in collection of S P Evans.

7 *Lancet*, 21 February 1903.

8 *Times*, 14, 20 November 1888.

9 PRO HO 65/62.

10 *Ibid.*

CHAPTER TEN – 13 MILLER'S COURT

1 *Weekly Dispatch*, 18 November 1888.

2 *Daily Telegraph*, 10 November 1888.

3 *Sunday Times*, 11 November 1888.

4 *England*, 17 November 1888.

5 *Weekly Dispatch*, 18 November 1888.

6 *Ibid.*

7 *Times*, 14 November 1888.

8 *Evening News* (London), 8 December 1888.

9 *Manchester Evening News*, 10 December 1888.

10 *Evening News* (London), 8 December 1888.

11 *Star*, 19 November 1888.

12 *Manchester Evening News*, 7 December 1888.

13 *Western Mail*, 7 December 1888.

14 *Northern Daily Telegraph*, 7 December 1888.

15 *Manchester Evening News*, 7 December 1888.

16 PRO CAB 41/21/17.

CHAPTER ELEVEN – THE GREAT SILK ROBBERIES

1   PRO CRIM 10/79, *Times*, 1, 8, 15, 22, 29 December 1888, 15, 16 January 1889.
2   *Sunday Times*, 23 December 1888.

CHAPTER TWELVE – 'CLAY PIPE' ALICE

1   All inquest reports taken from *Daily Telegraph*, *East London Advertiser*, *East London Observer*, *Lloyd's Weekly Newspaper* and the *Times*.
2   PRO HO 149/3.
3   *Daily Telegraph*, 19 July 1889.
4   *Evening News* (London), 23 July 1889.
5   *Pall Mall Gazette*, 4 November 1889.

CHAPTER THIRTEEN – THE PINCHIN STREET TORSO

1   'Heroes of the Police,' *Royal Magazine*, vol. 1, Nov 1898-Apr 1899.
2   *New York Herald*, 11 September 1889.
3   PRO MEPO 2/227.
4   *Morning Advertiser*, 25 September 1889.
5   *Morning Advertiser*, 30 September 1889.
6   *Morning Advertiser*, 1 October 1889.
7   *Pall Mall Gazette*, 16 April 1910.

CHAPTER FOURTEEN – THE LAST WHITECHAPEL MURDER

1   Bradford lost his arm after being attacked by a tiger in India. The tiger was killed and its teeth are on display at New Scotland Yard.
2   *Evening Standard*, 13 February 1891.
3   *Evening Standard*, 14 February 1891.
4   *Daily Chronicle*, 14 February 1891.
5   *Daily Telegraph*, 19, 20 February 1891.
6   *Daily Telegraph*, 18 February 1891.
7   *Ibid.*
8   *Morning Advertiser*, 16 February 1891.

9   *Weekly Dispatch*, 1, 8 March 1891.
10 *Herts & Cambs Reporter*, 20 March 1891.
11 *Weekly Dispatch*, 1 March 1891.
12 *London Metropolitan Archives*, ST/P/BG/162/015.
13 *East London Observer*, 28 March 1891.

Chapter Fifteen – Druids and Coiners

1   *East London Observer*, 5 September 1891.
2   *East London Observer*, 4 June 1892.
3   *Weekly Dispatch*, 8 March 1896.
4   *East London Observer*, 28 October 1893.
5   *East London Observer*, 25 November 1893.
6   PRO CRIM 10/84.
7   *Times*, 4 January 1894.
8   *Police Review and Parade Gossip*, 12 June 1896.
9   *Times*, 10 January 1894.

Chapter Sixteen – Retirements and Suspects

1   *Cassell's Saturday Journal*, 28 May 1892.
2   *East London Observer*, 11 June 1892.
3   *Ibid*.
4   *Eastern Post and City Chronicle*, 3 February 1893.
5   *East London Observer*, 20 May 1893.
6   PRO HO 395/1.
7   PRO MEPO 2/210.
8   N. Warren, 'The Arrest of Thomas Cutbush,' *Ripperana No. 4*, April 1993.
9   N. Connell, 'Colocitt,' *Ripperana No. 19*, January 1997.
10 *Sun*, 13-19 February 1894.
11 The case file on Thomas Hayne Cutbush, (held at Berkshire County Record Office), was opened to the public in November 2008 and shows that he was violent until his death in 1903. However the file contain nothing to indicate that he was suspected of being Jack the Ripper.
12 *Morning Leader*, 13 February 1894.

13 *Morning Leader*, 16 February 1894.

14 *Times*, 29 December 1888.

15 *Bristol Times and Mirror*, 11 February 1891.

16 *Western Mail*, 26 February 1892.

17 *Daily Mail*, 2 June 1913.

18 London Metropolitan Archives H12/CH/B2/2.

19 London Metropolitan Archives H12/CH/B13/39.

20 *Lloyd's Weekly Newspaper*, 15 December 1889.

21 *Police Gazette*, 26 October 1888.

22 PRO MEPO 6/15, *Times*, 20 December 1900.

23 *Police Review and Parade Gossip*, August 12, 1898. Race's pension record shows that he had been demoted to the rank of sergeant, (PRO MEPO 21/27).

24 *San Francisco Chronicle*, 23 November 1888.

25 *World* (New York), 29 January 1889.

26 *Dundee Advertiser*, 12 February 1889.

27 *Thomson's Weekly News*, 12 February 1927.

Chapter Seventeen – Reid's Ripper Reminiscences

1 PRO MEPO 21/25.

2 PRO MEPO 7/58.

3 PRO MEPO 4/340.

4 *Lloyd's Weekly News*, 4 February 1912.

5 PRO MEPO 21/25.

6 *Lloyd's Weekly Newspaper*, 8 March 1896.

7 *Herne Bay Press*, 8 December 1917.

8 *Lloyd's Weekly Newspaper*, 8 March 1896.

9 *Weekly Dispatch*, 8 March 1896.

10 *Police Review and Parade Gossip*, 12 June 1896.

11 *Herne Bay Press*, 27 September 1902.

12 *Lloyd's Weekly News*, 4 February 1912.

13 *Police Review and Parade Gossip*, 12 June 1896.

14 *Weekly Dispatch*, 3 August 1896.

15 *Sun*, 28 May 1901.

16 *Pall Mall Gazette*, 1 June 1901.

17 *Sun*, 31 May 1901.

18   *Eastern Post and City Chronicle*, 1 June 1901.

19   *East End News*, 14 June 1901.

20   *Eastern Post and City Chronicle*, 1 June 1901.

21   *East London Advertiser*, 1 June 1901.

22   *The People*, 2 June 1901.

23   PRO MEPO 3/162.

24   *East London Observer*, 1 June 1901.

25   *Pall Mall Gazette*, 24 March 1903.

26   *Pall Mall Gazette*, 31 March 1903.

27   *Morning Advertiser*, 24 March 1903.

28   *Morning Advertiser*, 30 March 1903.

29   *Ibid.*

CHAPTER EIGHTEEN – ANDERSON'S SUSPECT

1   *Cassell's Saturday Journal*, 11 June 1892.

2   *Windsor Magazine*, January-June 1895.

3   *Daily Chronicle*, 1 September 1908.

4   *Blackwood's Magazine*, March 1910.

5   *The People*, 24 March 1912.

6   Swanson's copy of Anderson's autobiography is now held at New
     Scotland Yard's Crime Museum. Dr Christopher Davies of the gov-
     ernment's Forensic Science Service analysed Swanson's notes in 2008.
     He reported that the annotations on the endpaper were made some
     years after the marginalia. (http://forensicsfaq.com/what-can-foen-
     sic-linguistics-tell-us-about-jack-the-ripper.html)

7   *Jewish Chronicle*, 4 March 1910.

8   *Globe*, 7 March 1910.

9   *Jewish Chronicle*, 11 March 1910.

10   PRO CRIM 10/85. This official publication deemed the details
     of the crime to be unfit for publication and only contain the
     verdict.

11   *Times*, 28 March 1895.

12   *Pall Mall Gazette*, 16 April 1910.

13   *Morning Advertiser*, 23 October 1910.

14   *East London Observer*, 14 May 1910.

Chapter Nineteen – The City Police Suspect

1 *Reynolds News*, 15 September 1946.
2 *Thomson's Weekly News*, 1 December 1906.

Chapter Twenty – Final Thoughts on the Ripper

1 *Eastern Post and City Chronicle*, 30 December 1911.
2 *East London Advertiser*, 17 February 1912.
3 *Eastern Post and City Chronicle*, 9 March 1912.
4 *Lloyd's Weekly News*, 4 February 1912.
5 *Pall Mall Gazette*, 2 April 1903.

Chapter Twenty-One – A Man of Kent

1 *Lloyd's Weekly News*, 4 February 1912.
2 Walter Jerrold, *Highways and Byways in Kent*, London, Macmillan and Co., 1908.
3 *Lloyd's Weekly News*, 4 February 1912.
4 *Herne Bay Press*, 29 September 1897.
5 *Herne Bay Press*, 19 June 1897.
6 *Herne Bay Press*, 26 June 1897.
7 *Herne Bay Press*, 10 October 1898. The Lower Red Lion ceased trading as a pub in 1920.
8 *Herne Bay Press*, 1 September 1900.
9 East Kent Archives Centre MH/T3/Mc11.
10 *Ibid.*
11 *Ibid.*
12 East Kent Archives Centre MH/T3/Kr4.
13 Mary Puta was the widow of Richard Puta, a printer who died in Whitechapel in 1893.
14 Centre for Kentish Studies IR4/86/2.
15 *Herne Bay Argus*, 5 May 1900. Despite the claim they were a good investment the houses fell victim to coastal erosion some sixteen years later.
16 Frank Mount, *My Recollections of Hampton*, Kent, 1942.
17 PRO HO 144/261; MEPO 3/153.

18 *Times*, 13-15 November 1894, 5 December 1894.

19 *East London Observer*, 9 May 1896.

20 *Thomson's Weekly News*, 19 November 1932.

21 *Herne Bay Press*, 27 September 1902.

CHAPTER TWENTY-TWO – KENTISH ADVENTURES

1 *Herne Bay Press*, 29 May 1897.

2 *Herne Bay Press*, 5 June 1897.

3 *Herne Bay Press*, 12 June 1897.

4 *Herne Bay Press*, 19 June 1897. Despite his differences over the years with local government figures Reid may have been involved with the Herne Parish Council. The Herne Parish Council Rough Minute Book 1895-1902 (ref. Canterbury Cathedral Archives PC10/A/1/1) includes an entry for 12th July 1898 saying 'Letter from Mr E Reid read asking council to allow him to resign respecting the office of Parish Cllr.' The newspaper account of the resignation said Councillor Reid resigned under 'pressure of business and circumstances over which he had no control.' He hoped his successor would 'do his utmost for 'good old Herne' which needed much improvement.' (*Herne Bay Press*, 16 July 1898). If this was Edmund Reid the resignation may have coincided with his wife's mental deterioration.

5 *Herne Bay Press*, 13 March 1899.

6 *Herne Bay Press*, 19 August 1899.

7 *Herne Bay Press*, 9 September 1899.

8 *Herne Bay Press*, 27 October 1900.

9 *Herne Bay Press*, 23 June 1900.

10 *Herne Bay Press*, 10 November 1900.

11 *Herne Bay Press*, 6 April 1901.

12 *Herne Bay Press*, 3 April 1909.

13 *Herne Bay Press*, 9 July 1910.

14 *Herne Bay Press*, 16 July 1910.

15 *Herne Bay Press*, 2 March 1912.

16 *Herne Bay Press*, 28 September; 2, 9 November 1912.

17 *Herne Bay Press*, 25 December 1915.

Chapter Twenty-Three – Building Bridges

1   *Herne Bay Press*, 16 August 1902.
2   *Herne Bay Press*, 12 August 1911.
3   *Herne Bay Press*, 20 July 1912.
4   *Thomson's Weekly News*, 29 March 1924.
5   *Herne Bay Press*, 9, 23 January 1909.
6   *Herne Bay Press*, 26 June, 25 September 1909.
7   *Herne Bay Press*, 12, 19 March, 30 April 1910.
8   *Herne Bay Press*, 19 March 1910.
9   *Herne Bay Press*, 28 May 1910.

Chapter Twenty-Four – Desecrating the Sabbath

1   *Herne Bay Press*, 1 October 1910.
2   *Herne Bay Press*, 8, 22 October 1910.
3   *Herne Bay Press*, 15 October 1910.
4   *Herne Bay Press*, 22 October 1910.
5   *Herne Bay Press*, 29 October 1910.
6   *Herne Bay Press*, 9 November 1912.
7   Reid also attached a sign by the remains of the Hampton village pump. In 1914 Reid's neighbour at Hampton, Mr. H.W. Carter wrote to the Board of Trade pleading for improved coastal defences but he was referred back to the local council. (Ref. PRO MT 10/1711).
8   *Morning Leader*, 2 March 1910.
9   *Herne Bay Press*, 8 December 1917. Dr T.A. Bowes became a noted local historian in Herne Bay and there is now a waxwork model of him on display at Herne Bay Museum.
10 *Ibid.*
11 *Herne Bay Press*, 15 December 1917.
12 *Hastings and St. Leonards Observer*, 15 January 1938.
13 Letter from Peter Day (Edmund Reid's great-grandson) to N. Connell, 17 September 1998.

Bibliography

BOOKS

Borough Guide to Herne Bay, 1909.

Robert Anderson, *The Lighter Side of My Official Life*, London, Hodder & Stoughton, 1910.

Mike Bundock (ed), *Historic Herne and Broomfield*, Kent, 2007.

Stewart P. Evans and Keith Skinner, *The Ultimate Jack the Ripper Sourcebook*, London, Constable & Robinson, 2000.

Charles Gibbon, *By Mead and Stream*, London, Chatto & Windus, 1884.

W.J. Gordon, *How London Lives*, London, Religious Tract Society, 1890.

John Heywood, *Illustrated Guide to Herne Bay and Neighbourhood*, London, 1903.

Walter Jerrold, *Highways and Byways in Kent*, London, Macmillan and Co., 1908.

Shane Leslie, *Sir Evelyn Ruggles-Brise*, London, John Murray, 1938.

Frank Mount, *My Recollections of Hampton, Kent*, 1942.

Philip Sugden, *The Complete History of Jack the Ripper*, New York, Carroll & Graf, 2002.

NEWSPAPERS AND PERIODICALS

Blackwood's Magazine

Bristol Times and Mirror

Cassell's Saturday Journal

Chelmsford Chronicle

Daily Chronicle
Daily Mail
Daily Telegraph
Dundee Advertiser
East End News
East London Advertiser
East London Observer
Eastern Post and City Chronicle
England
Evening News (London)
Evening News (Portsmouth)
Evening Standard
Globe
Hastings and St Leonards Observer
Herne Bay Argus
Herne Bay Press
Herts and Cambs Reporter
Illustrated Police News
Jewish Chronicle
Lancet
Lloyd's Weekly Newspaper
Manchester Evening News
Morning Advertiser

Morning Leader
New York Herald
Northern Daily Telegraph
Pall Mall Gazette
The People
Police Gazette
Police Review and Parade Gossip
Reynolds News
Ripperana
Royal Magazine
San Francisco Chronicle
Star
Star of the East
Sun
Sunday Times
Thomson's Weekly News
The Times
Toby
Weekly Dispatch
Western Mail
Windsor Magazine
World (New York)
Yarmouth Mercury

Index

Also available from Amberley Publishing

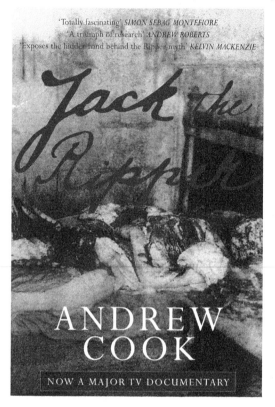

Finally lays to rest the mystery of who Jack the Ripper was

'Totally fascinating' SIMON SEBAG MONTEFIORE
'A triumph of research' ANDREW ROBERTS
'Exposes the hidden hand behind the Jack the Ripper myth' KELVIN MACKENZIE

The most famous serial killer in history. A sadistic stalker of seedy Victorian backstreets. A master criminal. The man who got away with murder – over and over again. But while literally hundreds of books have been published, trying to pin Jack's crimes on an endless list of suspects, no-one has considered the much more likely explanation for Jack's getting away with it... He never existed.

£9.99 Paperback
53 illustrations and 47 figures
256 pages
978-1-84868-522-2

Available from all good bookshops or to order direct
Please call **01453-847-800**
www.amberleybooks.com